1/6 Scale Stuart Tank

Large Scale Armor Modeling

Building a 1/6 Scale

STUART TANK

Making an Accurate Scale Model
from the 1/6 Scale
21st Century Toys™ Radio-Controlled M5A1
Stuart Light Tank

Robert N. Steinbrunn

Schiffer Military History
Atglen, PA

Dedication

I offer my heartfelt thanks to Barb–my best friend–who was supportive, tolerant, and patient throughout the almost-five years this project consumed. Her total lack of interest in things armored was most refreshing. Her encouragement for my doing what I enjoy as a hobby was most inspirational. Every modeler should have a wife like her.

Book Design by Ian Robertson.

Copyright © 2011 by Robert N. Steinbrunn.
Library of Congress Control Number: 2011934476

Printed in China.
ISBN: 978-0-7643-3953-0

We are interested in hearing from authors with book ideas on related topics.

Published by Schiffer Publishing Ltd.
4880 Lower Valley Road
Atglen, PA 19310
Phone: (610) 593-1777
FAX: (610) 593-2002
E-mail: Info@schifferbooks.com.
Visit our web site at: www.schifferbooks.com
Please write for a free catalog.
This book may be purchased from the publisher.
Please include $5.00 postage.
Try your bookstore first.

In Europe, Schiffer books are distributed by:
Bushwood Books
6 Marksbury Avenue
Kew Gardens
Surrey TW9 4JF, England
Phone: 44 (0) 20 8392-8585
FAX: 44 (0) 20 8392-9876
E-mail: Info@bushwoodbooks.co.uk.
Visit our website at: www.bushwoodbooks.co.uk
Try your bookstore first.

Contents

Acknowledgments.. 6

Foreword, *by Jim Mesko* 7

Regarding the Author, *by Jack Mugan*........................ 9

Introduction 10

Chapter 1: Background.. 11
How this project came about 11
Change of focus... 11
What if you can't find a 1/6 scale Stuart?............ 11
What to expect from this project 12
A snapshot in time - the markings
for this model 12

Chapter 2: Tools You'll Need 13

Chapter 3: Preliminary Preparations 14

Chapter 4: Hull Construction Starts 17

Chapter 5: Creating the Suspension Components
in Stages 23
Stage 1 - The drive sprockets 23
Stage 2 - The lower hull, Part A......................... 25
Stage 3 - The bogies 26
Stage 4 - The lower hull, Part B 36
Stage 5 - Final comments on the bogies............. 38
Stage 6 - Finishing up the final drive units......... 42
Stage 7 - The return rollers 42
Stage 8 - The idler wheels, arms,
and brackets.. 46

Chapter 6: The Air Deflectors 54
Scratch-building the lower air deflectors............. 54
Scratch-building the upper air deflector 55

Chapter 7: Finishing the Lower Hull...................... 56
Painting schedule outline.................................. 56
Painting schedule in detail................................. 56

Chapter 8: Creating the T16E1 Tracks
from Resin Castings 60

Chapter 9: Wiring up the Electronics 66

Chapter 10: Modifying the Upper Hull in Stages 70
Stage 1 - Fenders 70
Stage 2 - Headlights... 75
Stage 3 - Glacis plate.. 77
Stage 4 - Periscopes and hull hatches................. 78
Stage 5 - Hull midsection 83
Stage 6 - Forward engine deck 84
Stage 7 - Radiator caps and fuel
tank caps... 88
Stage 8 - Aft engine deck................................... 91
Stage 9 - Aft hull quarter panels 92
Making weld beads 92
Stage 10 - Aft hull plates 96

Chapter 11: Painting the Upper Hull...................... 98

Chapter 12: Turret Work Begins 104
Turret interior... 105
Turret hatches 111
Turret interior right sidewall...............................111
Turret interior left sidewall.................................111
Turret exterior rear plate.................................. 112
Turret roof exterior 113
Detailing the grousers...................................... 115
Turret wiring.. 117
Painting of interior turret components.............. 117
Turret exterior... 121
Upper air deflector.. 131
Working with stencils 131

Chapter 13: Final Assembly 134
Adding the turret... 134
Joining the upper and lower hulls...................... 135
Making Tie-down Straps 137
Adding final details.. 139
Finishing touches 140
Final thoughts 140

Chapter 14: Gallery - The M5A1 Stuart Light Tank
in 1/6 Scale............................... 141

Bibliography 162

Sources, Suppliers, and Online Resources.................... 164

About the author 166

Copyrights 168

Acknowledgments

A model such as this is never built in a vacuum, that is, in total isolation. There are many books, magazines, and websites I drew upon for information from the thousands of armor experts around the world. Armor modelers are truly a global community and I've learned much from them. If it's perceived by the reader that this model has a certain degree of quality, then I'd have to express my thanks to all the expert armor modelers out there who have shared what they know with the rest of us, helping us all to improve our work.

Thanks go to Kurt Laughlin–a man who knows more about the Stuart tank than I'll ever hope to learn–who patiently answered a number of queries over the course of this build and offered sound advice on the changes of the real M5A1 as production progressed. Serious M5/M5A1 Stuart builders will want a copy of his book *A Field Guide to the M5 Series Light Tanks and the M8 Howitzer Motor Carriage*, which is listed in the bibliography.

Thanks to Joe DeMarco–another expert on the Stuart tank–for his informative advice and help on the G103 Yahoo® group (M5A1 Stuart enthusiasts). Joe freely shared his comprehensive list *M5 AND M5A1 SERIAL NUMBER AND REGISTRATION NUMBER ASSIGNMENTS*, a valuable reference published on the G103 Yahoo® group from which I gathered much useful information.

Next, I drew the inspiration for the markings of this M5A1 model from Steven J. Zaloga's excellent book *Modelling the M3/M5 Stuart Light Tank*, which is listed in the bibliography. This title is highly recommended for anyone contemplating building any variant of the Stuart. In any scale.

I owe a debt of gratitude to Rob Ervin of Formations Models for his expertise in casting the hundreds of resin track blocks and end connectors. Rob is a gentleman of the "old school," and completion of the 1/6 M5A1 Stuart project was possible only because he agreed to take on this onerous casting job. It's probable this caused him nightmares and regret.

It is with great gratitude I thank my decades-long friend, artist, and modeling guru Jack Mugan for his frequent critiques of my work, and also for writing *Regarding the author*. Through Jack I've learned to associate *art* with *modeling*. I won't profess to have been able to combine the two as expertly as he has, but I keep trying.

Special thanks also go out to long-time friend Jim Mesko, one of the most authoritative armor experts and prolific authors in the field, not only for the foreword, but also for copies of hundreds of digital photographs taken during his thorough coverage of an M5A1 undergoing restoration. This prized collection of comprehensive and detailed photographs of M5A1 minutiae was a great aid in adding details and getting them right.

I am indebted to Bill Klingbiel for his invaluable (and seemingly endless) digital photographs of the same M5A1 undergoing restoration that supplemented Jim's and which proved priceless.

Another source of great reference photographs came from Chris "Toadman" Hughes. Chris' *M5A1 Stuart Walkaround CD*, which is listed in the bibliography, is highly recommended.

Foreword

by Jim Mesko

Since I began seriously modeling in the mid-1960s I have had the privilege and pleasure to meet a lot of very talented people in this hobby. Out of all of them, Bob Steinbrunn stands out as one of the best in the country. As you look over this book I am sure you will see why I feel this way.

I had the opportunity to meet Bob at an International Plastic Modelers' Society (IPMS) National Convention back in the late 1980s. I had seen Bob's work in several issues of *FineScale Modeler* magazine and was astounded at the level of detail he was able to put in 1/48 scale aircraft. Though my main interest is armor, Bob's aircraft articles provided the modeler with lots of techniques that were easily transferred over to *any* area of modeling. His attention to detail and accuracy showed what a dedicated builder could do with the most basic of materials and research to create a masterpiece. As we talked we found we shared a common background, both of us being Vietnam veterans with a love of modeling and history. Bob had served as a combat helicopter pilot, and I had been assigned to work with Vietnamese forces as part of the "Vietnamization" program.

That summer I was on vacation and was able to stop at Bob's home and see his models and workshop up close. Seeing both the finished product and projects under construction was an eye opening experience. At that time there were not a lot of aftermarket products available. Bob worked primarily with sheet plastic and wire to create some of the most beautifully detailed models I had ever seen. One project he had underway was a Monogram Models Dornier Do 335 that he was adding an interior to. It was so beautifully done that I told him it was a shame to paint it and cover up all that fantastic work. In his typical modest fashion Bob just smiled and said it wasn't really that much work and that it was nothing special.

For several IPMS conventions our paths crossed; we also stayed in touch at Christmas and through an occasional phone call. I heard through the grapevine that Bob had switched over to building wooden ship models. This made me glad, because I definitely did not want to have to compete with him in the armor

category in any IPMS competitions. We did share research material as both of us built on our Vietnam roots. Bob kept flying, working as an emergency medical service helicopter pilot for a hospital. I went into teaching and writing books in my spare time for Squadron/Signal Publications. I wrote numerous books based on information and photos I had acquired while in Vietnam, and Bob readily shared his supply of photos and proved very helpful in providing some unusual photographs I was able to use.

I didn't see Bob again until the 2006 IPMS National Convention in Kansas City, where I saw a beautifully detailed *Fletcher*-class destroyer, the U.S.S. *Kidd,* entered in competition. As I looked over the model I suspected Bob was the builder. When we met, he confirmed that it was his. The model was outstanding, the detail was astounding, and everything came together in a visually eye-catching model that people lined up to see. In recognition of his workmanship Bob was awarded the *George Lee Judges Grand Award* for the *Best in Show* model. This award is the highest honor any modeler in IPMS can achieve. It was named in honor of the late George Lee, who was an award-winning builder, but more importantly, who was a true gentleman and scholar. I was very happy that Bob had received this recognition, as he was truly deserving of it. Not only from the modeling aspect, but also because he exemplified the qualities that George exhibited as a fine human being.

I next saw Bob at the Armor Modeling and Preservation Society (AMPS) National Convention at Havre de Grace in 2009. Bob had decided to start building armor. There he showed me the beginnings of the project that this book spotlights. By coincidence I was working at that time on a Squadron/Signal Walk Around book on the M5/M5A1 Stuart light tank. As we talked and shared our current projects, we realized that we could help each other out. What followed was a huge transfer of photos from each of our files dealing with the M5 and M5A1. I had access to one that was being completely restored from the ground up, while Bob had an extensive collection of M5 and M5A1 photographs of those under restoration and various ones on display in museums. I was able to use several of his photos in my book; in turn he was able to glean details from my photographs that appeared on his model.

What follows here is a great primer for anyone who enjoys building models, no matter what their area of interest. The level of detail and research found on the model in this book exemplify the highest building skills in this hobby. There is much in the pages that follow that will be of benefit for every modeler. And that, I think, will make Bob very happy, because he has always been willing to share his ideas and skills with his fellow modelers. That is the type of individual he is. I consider it the greatest of honors to have been able to write this introduction for a fellow Vietnam veteran, an outstanding modeler, but more importantly, a good friend.

Jim Mesko is an internationally-recognized author who has written over 30 books relating to aircraft, armor, and the Vietnam War. Jim is also an accomplished modeler who has won many awards for his aircraft and armor models in IPMS and AMPS national competitions.

Regarding the Author

by Jack Mugan

As a long time modeler and his number one fan I appreciate this opportunity to introduce to you my good friend Bob Steinbrunn. First and foremost, to me Bob is a modeler's modeler, a photographer, and a gentleman. He is also a great mentor to all who look to him for guidance, knowledge, and inspiration. Bob has achieved high recognition through his numerous build articles found in a wide variety of model magazines, as well as the many awards for his modeling efforts. In the world of modeling he is nothing short of a superstar to many who follow his work.

Bob and I met many years ago when we were both members of the Twin Cities Aero Historians, located in Minneapolis/St. Paul, Minnesota. The club, whose main focus was the love of aviation, attracted modelers, writers, artists, collectors and photographers, and enjoyed a rather large membership. As TCAH fellow members for many years, Bob and I traveled to museums and model competitions around the country. Bob continued to focus on his modeling skills while I became more involved with club activities. I did all right in model competition but he excelled.

Bob flew Hueys in Vietnam and liked to say he survived the experience. While he received an impressive number of decorations for his service to his country, he seldom talked about that time in his life. However once, on a trip to Washington, DC, I recall him pointing to the names engraved in the wall of the Vietnam Memorial, saying that listed there was much of the flight school class he trained with. Bob always had a camera with him in combat and returned home with an impressive photo journal of his Army flying experiences, many that he used in his Squadron/Signal publication *Vietnam Scrapbook*.

Bob's early models, though well built, were nothing like he builds today. Over time, as he developed his considerable modeling skills, the models became extremely detailed as he began moving into scratch building. His personal challenge became taking each project to its full potential. For the next several years Bob's interests were focused on World War II aircraft subjects in 48th scale. Once he felt he had mastered this venue to his satisfaction he turned his interest to ship modeling.

This dramatic change in modeling direction brought many new challenges, as well as the need to develop a new skill set. The time required to complete a ship model to his standards meant that each project was now going to take years to construct, and keeping focused would require discipline and patience. Just as with his aircraft projects, Bob spent much of his time gathering information as well as keeping a photo journal and a log of his work's progress. Starting out with a sailing ship, he learned about planking and making his own lines and so much more. After several years of in-progress articles the project was finally completed and began winning recognition in model competition.

The next project was to be a World War II destroyer that was a completely different kind of ship modeling. No more sails, planks and lines. Now instead of wood there was steel plating. Bob said that unlike aircraft, where much of the detail is internal, the detail on steel warships is on the outside, and there was plenty of detail to be had on his destroyer project. Once again, the building pattern of buying a kit of a subject and then replacing ninety percent of the kit-supplied parts with his own became the challenge. Here was a project that allowed Bob to bring his scratch building skills and attention to detail from building aircraft and apply it to this project, which would take five years to reach completion. The destroyer achieved national attention through model magazine articles and captured many major model awards around the country.

Then one day his attention was drawn to a large scale tank model, and of course he had a need to dismantle it and make his own improvements. And so began the next chapter in Bob's modeling experience. As you will see in this book, Bob has once again brought his considerable talent and attention to detail to bear, not only in a different venue, but also in a new scale from his previous experience. I believe you will enjoy it.

Jack Mugan is a former commercial artist, advertising director, and media director whose extensive background in art has been the basis of the exquisite models he builds. Jack is past president of the Twin City Aero Historians in Minneapolis (a chapter of IPMS), and current president of IPMS Gainesville, Florida. Jack is a prolific writer of modeling articles and has won a number of awards for his models in IPMS competitions.

Introduction

The one-sixth scale hobby is growing rapidly and is becoming more popular each year. A bewildering array of items is available to the 1/6 scale enthusiast, and new releases seem to appear almost daily from a growing list of main-line and "cottage industry" manufacturers. The complexity, accuracy, and detail of many of these figures, vehicles, and various accessories are now attracting the attention of a number of scale modelers who have previously overlooked this sector of modeling. Some of the weapons, for example, operate, look, feel, and disassemble much like the originals. Some of the large metal armored vehicles have features and price tags which take them far from the realm of toys. In short, this has become a fascinating field of large scale models which incorporate such vast amounts of detail that they are converting many former small-scale modelers to this large scale.

A project like this will be a very unusual experience for the first-time 1/6 scale builder. Because the model and its parts are so big, one soon gets an eerie sense of working on the real thing. One aspect of modeling in this sizable scale is its unforgiving nature. By this I mean in the sense that everything is so big compared to, say, a 1/35 armor model, that no longer can you suggest complex components or parts by generic details or artistic sleight-of-hand. Even smaller parts are so large and visible in this scale that you actually have to build the parts themselves, right down to the safety lock wire securing drilled-out bolt heads, for instance. This is out of the ordinary for smaller scale models, and that makes this large scale an unusual sector of modeling. But it's all part of the fun and appeal of large-scale armor, and fortunately–since the parts are so big–they're relatively easy to make, handle, and detail.

Sticking with it

Another aspect of large-scale armor modeling is the length of time it takes to complete a project in this scale. A 1/35 armor model is 1/35th the size of the real vehicle, and on the model about 1/3 of an inch (8.709 millimeters) equals one foot on the original. A 1/6 scale model is much larger, where two inches on the model (50.80 mm) equal one foot on the original. This means the 1/6 scale model is almost six times larger than its 1/35 scale counterpart; consequently, the modeler can expect the 1/6 scale project to take about six times longer to complete than a 1/35 scale model. One way of maintaining interest in the project during this lengthy period of time is to view each completed component of the model as a model within itself. For example, completing the suspension components and having them painted, weathered, and finished gives a sense of completion equivalent to finishing a smaller model. Completing the lower hull's construction, painting, and weathering makes one feel as if another smaller model is finished. Completing the upper hull, turret, weapons, accessories, and stowage, each in turn, will create within the modeler the feeling that the project is moving right along and that progress is steadily being made. A very necessary feeling, indeed, if the modeler is to maintain interest in the project and see it through to completion over an extended period of time.

As time goes by you'll see the project slowly taking shape as things come together. If this rate of progress seems too slow for you and you become bored with what you're currently doing, you may find your interest level can be maintained by working on different components. You might see that working with white metal castings, brass rod and sheet brass, styrene rod and sheet styrene, and other materials keeps you interested, since there is always some new material, operation, procedure, or technique which makes the project seem like there's always something new to do. Whether you're building, painting, airbrushing, wiring, soldering, weathering, researching, or whatever particular aspect of armor modeling you're in at that moment, you'll engage in a wide variety of techniques over the course of the project. You'll find this fascinating, I believe, and generally speaking, this will help to keep your interest up for the long haul.

1

Background

How this project came about

Being a scale modeler who enjoys models of all types, I found myself attracted to a large semi-scale model of an M5A1 Stuart light tank released several years ago by 21ˢᵗ Century Toys™. I thought it might be fun to indulge in a radio controlled tank, and I thought perhaps I might be able to improve its scale appearance along the way. I was further enchanted with this project when I discovered the extensive line of aftermarket accessories and upgrade options available for this particular "model" from a number of cottage industry suppliers. The prospect of this now became very interesting and I knew I had to do it. But when I decided to go ahead with this project I found this toy was no longer in production and was unavailable in stores. Indeed, the manufacturer is now no longer in business, and I had to acquire my M5A1 from an online auction site, a method which carries with it some degree of risk. When the carton arrived, however, I found it was in undamaged condition, the box within was unopened, and the model inside was in new condition. I felt it was my lucky day and I was ready to start.

Change of focus

After taking the tank out of the box when it arrived and looking at it with a critical modeler's eye I began to see lots of room for improvement. I soon changed my focus from having a radio controlled toy which would be given a better scale appearance to that of making this toy into a "museum piece" which would occasionally be run. That is to say, it would be transformed into an accurate scale model as a primary goal with a secondary one of occasionally demonstrating its operating features to friends. The exact reverse of why I bought it in the first place.

I wasn't aware when I began what this project would eventually involve in terms of time, effort, and expense. Perhaps that was a good thing, or I might never have started. Still, having said that, I thoroughly enjoyed this project and I'd do it again. Was I successful in my goal of creating a scale museum model from a toy? I think I was, mostly, but I'll let the reader decide to what degree. Did I have fun along the way? Absolutely, and I feel that's the true benchmark of success for a long-term hobby project like this one.

What if you can't find a 1/6 scale Stuart?

In this presentation the M5A1 light tank is merely serving in the role of a demonstrator model in order to illustrate to the reader the many processes, procedures, materials, and techniques which are applicable to *all* types of large-scale armor models. Even if you're not building an M5A1 Stuart–or even a model in 1/6 scale–hopefully you'll find something of value here for your own armor project, whether it's a scratch-build, a modification of a finished and ready-to-display model, or an upscale all-metal radio-controlled kit. If this book helps the reader even a little bit with his or her own project, it will then have served its purpose.

The 21st Century Toys™ Stuart as it comes from the box. Basically a toy (as may easily be seen), it has great potential for becoming a scale model since it's dimensionally accurate. It will just take time and effort.

What to expect from this project

The 21st Century Toys™ M5A1 Stuart tank, as it comes out of the box, provides a good starting point for an accurate model, given time, patience, and good reference material. Be prepared for many modeling challenges, since there are a number of things that have to be changed, corrected, or eliminated. Other challenges are inherent in working with different media, such as plastic, brass, white metal, and resin. Your skills may be challenged by the need to perform various operations, such as milling, lathing, wiring, soldering, airbrushing, and so on. But be prepared also for an enjoyable experience building in this large scale, however far you take your particular model or whatever your capabilities, tools, and equipment allow.

A snapshot in time–the markings for this model

It's always more interesting for me if the model I'm working on represents something specific rather than a generic nondescript tank. I was intrigued by Steve Zaloga's model of *Cognac* illustrated in *Modelling the M3/M5 Stuart Light Tank*, especially since there was a splash of color in the yellow 'C-32' tactical marking and the white markings representing data for loading it on board a ship

which appear on both sides of the hull. I thought this would add more visual interest to a solid Olive Drab vehicle and make the model more appealing. As nearly as I can tell from the various references listed in the bibliography, the markings on this model represent a mid-production M5A1 with this assignment:

Cognac
Company C, 3rd Battalion, 33rd Armored Regiment
3rd Armored Division
Saint-Fromond, France, 7 July 1944

This unit took part in the fighting during the crossing of the River Vire.

By noting the configuration and production features on this M5A1, then finding an appropriate registration number from Joe DeMarco's list, it's conceivable this tank was built at the Cadillac South Gate plant near Los Angeles, California, in February 1943. If this is so, based on the United States Army Registration number of 3046392, its serial number would have been 2958 and it would have been the 138th of 150 M5A1s built that month by South Gate.

2

Tools You'll Need

By virtue of the fact you're reading this, I think it's logical to assume you have already been in the armor hobby for some time, and if so, you've probably built 1/35 scale armor models. This being the case, it's also logical to assume you already have a stable of hand tools, paints, and brushes. This assortment of items is basically all you'll need. Possibly you own an airbrush with a source of air, which in most cases will be a hobby compressor. Large-scale armor models can be painted easily using spray cans if you wish, but I think most serious armor modelers will already have an airbrush on hand because of its ease of use and the quality of the finish this important tool brings to your project. Complex camouflage patterns–World War II German multi-colored ones for example–can realistically be done no other way.

Certain other power tools will enhance your ability to scratch-build certain parts and components and will speed up construction. These aren't strictly necessary to have, but if you have them already you'll find that you use them quite a bit. These include a small table saw, which is handy for cutting thick sheet styrene and also brass sheet up to about .050" in thickness. This thickness will vary according to the brand of saw you have and the particular blade you have installed. There are a number of fine saws on the market to choose from. In my case I had a Preac Micro-Precision Table Saw™ on hand which was used a great deal for this project.

Another tool I already had was a Sherline™ lathe, a small modeler's unit which allowed me to do certain turning operations which would have proved difficult to accomplish using hand tools. Not vital to have, certainly, but very handy and useful. I don't think I would have bought one just for this project, but having already had it I found I used it frequently and was very glad to have it around.

Modelers desiring further details on tools and materials might consider looking into various other armor modeling books listed in the bibliography for ideas on how to equip their workbench.

3

Preliminary Preparations

Since we're going to be discussing how to build upon and make this "kit" better, it's important to note that we must first make it *into* a kit. This means complete and total disassembly. This will be necessary in order to modify and detail the parts just as you would for any large scale plastic armor model kit, which is exactly what this will become. I felt it was vital to tag all parts with office labels, place all screws into compartmented trays with labels, and to occasionally make sketches of how things came apart so I wouldn't be embarrassed when I would need to get them back together again. I knew this project might take several years and I couldn't rely on my memory for that length of time. I also used short strips of masking tape to label all wires and connectors to make certain everything would be reconnected correctly. After complete disassembly I counted 462 parts, pieces, and screws–a not inconsiderable number–so it's wise to tag everything. Since we're reducing this model to a "kit", we'll refer to it as a *kit* henceforth.

The disassembled upper and lower hull sections ready for cutting and modifications. This is a large model, and you'll need lots of workbench space.

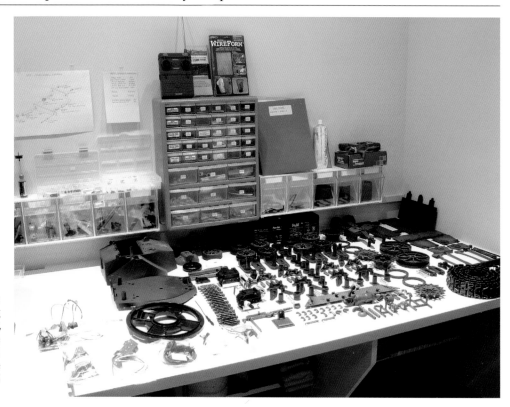

The disassembled model: parts laid out in a logical sequence and grouped according to function. There are no "kit" instructions, so it pays to stay organized to avoid the "Now, where does *this* go?" question. All of the screws and fasteners which were removed were sorted out into partitioned parts boxes and labeled.

A large workbench was necessary to lay out the parts in an organized fashion. Besides labeling the parts, all of the electronic components were placed in plastic zipper lock bags for protection from dust and were labeled. Inexpensive parts cabinets proved useful for organizing and storing the many aftermarket accessories and hardware items needed.

The tank breaks down into 462 pieces, which should be laid out in an organized manner if you expect to get it back together again. Organization also means cataloging aftermarket parts and accessories into the parts cabinet seen in the background.

The electrical motors, gearboxes, and drive train components were cleaned, lubricated, and reinstalled in proper alignment. The alignment of these items is important to check since it can be off by a wide margin, causing difficulties during operation.

The electrical motors, gearboxes, and drive train components were cleaned, lubricated, and reinstalled true to each other and to the hull. The proper alignment of these items is important to check, since it can be off by a wide margin, which will cause difficulties during operation. Washers to act as shims and some positional adjustments are all that are needed here. For lubricants I used Mobil 1™ synthetic grease and Woodland Scenics® Premium Gear Lube, since neither will degrade plastic parts. It's helpful if you have a computer near your workbench for ease of reference to the many photographs and other information you're certain to gather during the course of your project. I found it invaluable, and often printed out color photos of certain full-scale items and components I was duplicating in miniature in order to have a ready reference on my workbench next to the items I was working on. I also found it helpful to have an inexpensive drafting table in my shop which was used for many purposes: drafting, sketching, cutting stencils, holding books open for reference by my workbench, trimming decals, and so on. Having enough space in your shop for all this makes the project much more enjoyable.

4

Hull Construction Starts

All ejection pin marks and flash were sanded off, and all unauthentic seams, sinkholes, and joints were filled with 3M™ Acryl Green™ body putty or Milliput® two-part epoxy putty. Since this is a large model requiring heavy applications of filler in many places, I soon found myself using Milliput much more often than body putty since it doesn't shrink or crack like putty, which will require additional sanding, coats, and attention when any of these undesirable things happen. Milliput won't attack or soften the plastic like lacquer-based putty does, and it dries hard enough to drill and tap. It will easily accept screws and bolts if they're not run in too tightly.

The unauthentic aft extensions of the hull side plates and the spring guide housings mounted on these (which were located on the lower hull rear and side) for the idler wheel spring suspension were all cut away and sanded smooth. An Electro-File™ with a saw blade attachment was useful for making the larger and rougher cuts. Six unauthentic reinforcement brackets under the fenders were also cut away. Two unauthentic circular guides around the base of each of the six return rollers on the lower hull side were ground off. A number of unauthentic cooling and assembly slots in the lower hull sides, front, rear, and underneath were filled with sheet styrene and putty, including the louvers in the hull bottom for the acoustical speaker. The speaker was mounted in a new internal location in the engine compartment, a more authentic location for engine noise. Two unauthentic storage compartment doors on the hull bottom were cemented shut and their seams were filled.

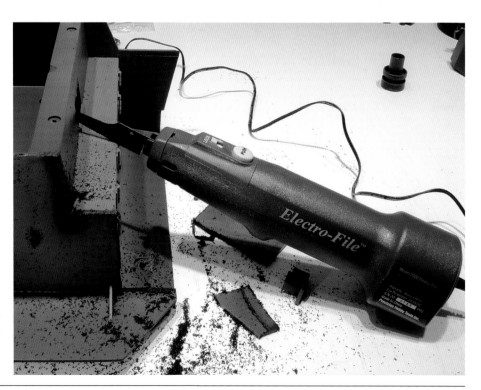

An Electro-File oscillating tool with a saw blade makes easy work of cutting off unauthentic toy features. Here the aft areas of the lower hull's side plates are being removed. These unauthentic sections mount the toy's simplified idler wheel spring assemblies.

Modifications to the bow: the contour of the final drive castings was too flat and angular. It was a simple matter to create rounded contours with .040" sheet styrene and Milliput epoxy putty. The slots where the Culin hedgerow device attaches were used to mount Armorpax white metal tow lugs. These were blended in to the hull with Milliput and 3M Acryl-Green body putty.

The two final drive housings on the nose of the hull inboard of the drive sprockets were too straight and flat in profile view and had sharp angular edges. A more realistic rounded contour was fashioned with sheet styrene super glued in a curved bow shape over a piece of brass tubing which was attached transversely to the flat fender under the sheet styrene. Milliput epoxy and acrylic body putty were used to soften and blend the contours in to make this assembly appear as a realistic casting. The underside of the nose had its contours revised by adding a half-round styrene strip transversely at the front of the hull bottom and blending it in with body putty. Each side of the housing has five holes drilled which have recessed plates made from .020" sheet styrene within, and four of these in turn are drilled and tapped to accept 2-56 hex head

bolts, while the two center holes have 00-80 bolts. The four 2-56 bolts each have six holes drilled in their heads to accept safety lock wire made from strands of copper AC electrical wire. The kit's Culin Hedgerow device was eliminated, and the slots in the lower front hull plate for mounting this were used instead to mount two white metal towing lugs from Armorpax™. The rear towing lugs were cut and filed to an authentic angled-corner shape from their original square shape and have weld beads made from Milliput epoxy putty all around their perimeters.

The kit's towing pintle was toy-like and was replaced. The cylindrical extension from the rectangular mount to the hook was cut off and a new one was made on a Sherline lathe from 1" solid brass rod. Two wing-like mechanical stops on the lower aft edge of the extension were cut from .030" brass sheet. These limit the arc the hook can swivel in. The end of the extension was bored out to accept an Armorpax tow hook mounted on two sizes of telescoping K & S® brass tubing which allow it to swivel. The hook was detailed with a release handle which was filed down to a tapered section, the inside perimeter of the lever was relieved with a ball cutter for authenticity, and a small ring cut from brass tubing was attached inside the larger ring. The pintle jaw as molded is much too thin, so it was built up to a scale thickness with Milliput. The rectangular mount was drilled and tapped to accept four 2-56 hex-head brass bolts with washers for realism. This assembly is a vast improvement on the kit's pintle.

Foundry casting numbers were added on the lower sections of the pintle, and were made by cutting part numbers from sprue runners from plastic kits and attaching them with Testors® liquid cement. The two lifting hooks on the lower hull sides were cut from .120" sheet styrene using a jigsaw plugged into a Dremel® speed control (rheostat) and run at a slow enough speed to avoid melting the plastic. These were roughly shaped with a milling cutter driven by a Dremel tool, then final-shaped with files and sandpaper. The hooks were attached to their mounting pads with a length of brass rod mounted in a hole drilled in the pad. The mounting pads each had four old-style rivet heads and two unauthentic plinths ground

The kit's pintle was too toy-like and was replaced. I cut off the extension from the rectangular mount and made a new one from 1" solid brass rod on my Sherline lathe. Two wing-like mechanical stops were cut from .030" brass sheet, and the end was bored out to accept an Armorpax tow hook mounted on two sizes of brass tubing to allow it to swivel.

The tow hook is mounted in the lathed brass extension and will swivel left and right until the bar on its undersurface contacts one of the wing-like mechanical stops. The hook functions like the real one does and is seen here with the toy's original hook.

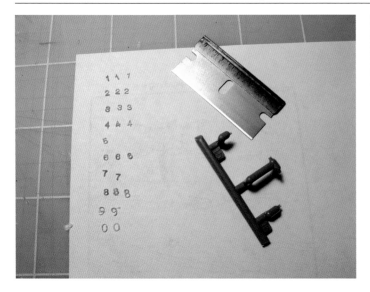

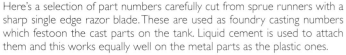

Here's a selection of part numbers carefully cut from sprue runners with a sharp single edge razor blade. These are used as foundry casting numbers which festoon the cast parts on the tank. Liquid cement is used to attach them and this works equally well on the metal parts as the plastic ones.

The model lacked the side hull lifting hooks and had some sort of plinths molded on the hooks' attaching pads instead. These plinths were ground off, along with the four old-style rivets molded on each pad. Two lifting hooks were drawn on .120" sheet styrene and were cut out on a jigsaw which was run slowly to avoid melting the plastic.

off prior to attaching the hooks, and each has a weld bead made from Milliput putty around its perimeter. The weld seams on the hull sides and bottom were made from Milliput epoxy putty. Thinly rolled strips of this were laid on slots cut in with a disk bur, and were tamped down and textured like a lapped arc weld in a realistic manner by use of a dental spatula. A home-made weld lapping tool for smaller weld lines was made from a section of brass tubing that was cut and shaped, then mounted on a paint brush handle. For more detail on this process see "Making weld beads" in Chapter 10.

The bottom of the hull was detailed with additional structural members made up as laminations of strip styrene. Various panels, access plates, and covers were made from sheet styrene in various thicknesses ranging from .040" up to .080". Many of these have drilled holes accommodating brass hex-head bolts in four sizes: 2-56, 1-72, 0-80, and 00-90 from Walthers® and Micro Fasteners™. The bolts are run into drilled and tapped holes, and many have

nuts and washers. The crew escape hatch was made similar to the other panels and is secured by brass flat-head screws driven into countersunk holes. The hatch is protected by bullet splash guards made up of styrene angle and triangular strip placed around its perimeter. Tack welds on many of the structural pieces were done with Milliput putty. Nine of the bolt heads towards the front of the hull bottom were drilled for and are locked by safety wire which was made from strands taken from AC electrical wire. There was an unauthentic opening on the hull front above the nose casting and under the glacis plate. A realistic countersunk lip structure was fashioned from .080" sheet styrene and has fillets made from .100" x .080" styrene strip laminated together. The glacis plate strip under the forward row of ten bolts was made from .040" sheet styrene and has counter-bored holes which accommodate ten 2-56 brass hex-head bolts with washers and nuts underneath. This replicates how the upper hull front deck plate and lower hull section were fastened together on the actual tank.

The hull bottom with its various hatches, access panels, structural members, drain valves, bolts, nuts, washers, weld beads, and other details added. The acoustical speaker has been removed from the hull bottom and relocated to the engine bay. The speaker's louvers in the hull bottom have been filled.

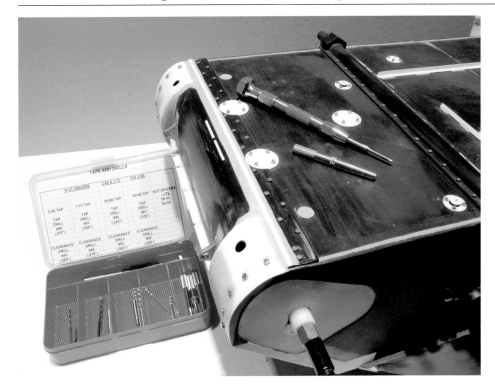

A craft box holds the four taps, their clearance and tap drills, the pin vise to drive the taps, and the four nut drivers. These are in sizes (large to small): 2-56, 1-72, 0-80, & 00-90. The many bolts, nuts, and washers in the model made the acquisition of these tools very necessary.

I acquired four taps, four tap drills, four clearance drills, and four nut drivers in sizes (large to small) 2-56, 1-72, 00-80, and 00-90 for installing the scale brass hardware. I also bought a swivel-handle pin vise which is ideal for driving the taps with less effort and more accuracy. An inexpensive compartmented parts box from the craft store made an ideal storage container for these tools. Labeling the nut drivers with different colors of tape made selecting the right one easy with just a glance.

Various hull drains and fittings were fashioned of sheet styrene, brass rod, and brass hardware. A number of bolt heads were drilled out for the later installation of lock wire.

A view of the hull bottom illustrating a row of bolts on the left, the middle four of which have had their heads drilled for safety lock wire which will be added later. Moving to the right we see two hull drain valves (both of which are open), and an access panel for the transfer unit oil drain valve.

At the left may be seen a Dremel Moto-tool mounted in a routing accessory. This was used to rout out the recess in the hull sides where the final drive units will be located. Sheet styrene .100" thick was used to fill in the missing sections of the hull sides on the forward top edge, shown white here. Under the sponson floors may be seen the weld bead made from Miliput epoxy putty.

Both hull sides inboard of the drive sprockets were routed out with a Dremel Moto-Tool™ mounted in a Dremel routing accessory in order to produce a recessed area inboard of the final drive units. Evergreen™ sheet styrene of .120" thickness was used to fill open areas of the forward edges of the hull sides. This view also shows how the profile of the final drive casting was expanded into a rounded curve from the kit's flat shape.

A Waldron™ Precision Punch & Die Set was used to punch out hundreds of styrene and brass disks for various uses. This is one of modeling's great tools.

A Waldron Punch & Die Set was used to punch out perfect disks in various thicknesses for a myriad of uses on the model.

An easy way of drilling out the many bolt heads which were secured by safety lock wire was to mount them in my Preac vise, center punch each of the six flats on the bolt head, then drill six holes with a #79 drill bit using a Dremel mounted in its drill press.

Dozens of brass bolt heads had to be drilled out for the addition of safety lock wire. This was done using a Dremel tool mounted in a Dremel drill press while the bolt to be drilled was held in a Preac vise. The brass used by Walthers for their bolts is much softer than that used by Micro Fasteners and made drilling the holes much easier and quicker with far fewer broken drill bits.

The final drive units were built up with sections of an amber plastic pill bottle, and each has six gussets made of .040" sheet styrene. The pinion gear housing was made from .100" sheet styrene and has details made of various thicknesses of the same material. 36 brass bolts in 1-72 size were screwed into drilled and tapped holes replicating where the final drive units were bolted to the controlled differential. Thirty-four of these bolts have their heads drilled out for safety lock wire, which was made from strands of AC electrical wire. White glue was used to create fillets in between all angular surfaces to round them out and blend them in so as to appear as a casting.

This shows how the final drive units were created after routing out the hull, filling the recessed area with sheet styrene, and fabricating all the pieces of the final drive units. Note the lock wire on three of the bolts placed here as an example of how all the bolts will be safety-wired.

5

Creating the Suspension Components in Stages

Stage 1 - The drive sprockets

The two front drive sprockets were modified from the kit's early open scalloped type to the later solid plate type. Both types of sprocket had 14 teeth. In 1942 the sprockets were redesigned to have a 2-inch smaller diameter with a different drive ratio, and these sprockets had only 13 teeth. I didn't have the difficult job of converting my sprockets to a 13-tooth configuration since they would still be accurate if I left them as 14-tooth types after converting them to the solid plate style, since both types were in use for a time.

The first step was to run a strip of .010" x .030" Evergreen strip styrene around the inside diameter of the drive teeth, creating a circle. This became the inside finished edge of the drive sprocket's tooth plate and also acted as a dam while I filled all 14 openings in each of the four plates with Miliput epoxy putty. The drive teeth were reshaped to the late style by using a ¼" cutting bur in my Dremel tool to cut a concave scallop on both sides of each tooth and enlarging and rounding the concavity at the bottom between each tooth. The original drive sprocket's track teeth had a convex curve to their shape which was changed to concave using the cutting bur. The 1-72 bolts holding the sprocket plates to the hub were screwed into holes which were drilled and tapped, protruding just a bit on the other side.

The eight spoke-like reinforcing gussets in the middle of each hub were overly thick, and were ground off along with the round nuts near the center. New gussets made of .040" sheet styrene were made for each sprocket, and eight 2-56 brass hex head bolts were run into drilled and tapped holes from the inside of the hub. Brass nuts and washers were then added to the protruding bolts. Four lengths of .010" styrene rod were added to the hub to replicate foundry casting seams. These were sanded down and slightly dissolved with liquid cement to make them partially blend in with the hub casting.

Foundry casting numbers and marks were added from sprue and a Lion Roar™ sheet of photoetch letters and numbers (*1:35 Metal Number For Surface Foundry Number Insignia*, part number *LAM042*). I actually bought eight of these photoetch sheets since I knew I had quite a few foundry casting numbers and tire markings to add in various sizes over the entire model. I used a sharp X-ACTO™ #11 knife blade to cut the letters and numbers from their fret, and did so within a clear plastic bag to prevent their loss at the moment of parting. Each letter and number then had to have its attaching stub carefully removed with a sanding stick while being held in a pair of self-closing tweezers. To attach these brass letters and numbers to the model I used liquid cement if joining them to plastic and white PVA (polyvinyl acetate) glue (Elmer's® brand in the U.S.) if attaching them to brass or white metal. These adhesives are good for giving you some working time to get the numbers in perfect alignment but are not permanent solutions. For permanency I overcoated the line of numbers with a layer of thin cyanoacrylate (CA) glue which locked them in place. When dry, a delicate rubbing with a sanding stick took off the sharp edges of the letters and numbers and blended them in to their background, giving them more of a foundry-cast look.

One of the front drive sprockets after converting it to the solid-plate late style from the earlier scalloped open-plate style which is shown on the right. There are 133 pieces in each sprocket. The two rings in the background are for retaining the unauthentic tracks with center guides and are simply removed and discarded.

Prior to assembling the two halves of each drive sprocket I removed and discarded the two rings sandwiched between the halves. These are guides for the unauthentic center-guide tracks and detract from the scale appearance of the sprockets. The deletion of these rings leaves prominent shoulders on the hub which I tapered down using my Sherline lathe. After creating an authentic hub taper by mounting each sprocket half on the lathe and turning down the shoulders the sprocket halves were joined. I added eight fillets transversely across each hub using Evergreen .060" x .080" strip styrene. These had their inside surfaces tapered to shape before and their outside edges blended to the hub after cementing them in position. Each sprocket has 105 pieces.

The drive sprocket being given the foundry rough-cast texture by the stippled application of Gunze Sangyo Mr. Surfacer 500. Reference material released later in the project would reveal an error seen here: the outer line of 14 bolts should be centered on the throats of the drive teeth rather than on the teeth themselves. I had no choice but to remove the bolts, fill the holes, and drill and tap new holes in the proper locations. Fifty-six times.

The sprockets were given a coat of Gunze Sangyo™ Mr. Surfacer 500™. This is a lacquer-based liquid putty which is stippled on with an old flat brush ¼" wide in order to replicate the texture of the rough-cast foundry finish. It's best to do just a small area at a time, cleaning the brush frequently with lacquer thinner, as the putty builds up on the bristles. A thorough cleaning when finished will save the brush for further use. This view of the drive sprocket in my hand gives you some idea of the sheer size of this model. Kurt Laughlin's book, which was published after the sprockets had reached this point in their assembly, gave me a nasty surprise–no fault of Kurt's. This excellent reference showed I had the outer 14 bolts incorrectly located. They should have been centered on the throats of the teeth rather than on the teeth themselves. I hadn't realized that there were four different types of drive sprockets for the M5A1 until this point. To recreate the late type 14-tooth sprocket with a solid toothed plate (which appeared prior to the later 13-tooth sprocket) meant I had to remove all 56 of them from the sprockets, fill the holes, re-drill and tap the new holes, and then repaint the sprockets. A fair amount of work and one of modeling's "little adventures", but I felt better for having done it, knowing I was taking the model to the highest level of accuracy my skills would allow. Many thanks to Kurt for his invaluable book full of M5 esoterica and details which is listed in the bibliography.

Stage 2 - The lower hull, Part A

The undersides of both sponsons were detailed with nuts, bolts, and washers which were used to fasten down equipment inside the full-size tank. Covers for the fuel tank drain valves were fashioned from Evergreen .080" sheet styrene and are bolted in place with 1-72 brass hex-head bolts, nuts, and washers located in routed-out recesses. Foundry casting numbers "A 456" were added from the Lion Roar sheets. The covers for the engine air cleaner access were also fashioned from .080" sheet styrene and are detailed with weld beads made from Milliput. The attaching means for these covers were cut from .040" sheet styrene.

Inboard of each bogie on the hull sides are two vertical pieces of L-angle strips which are guides for the inboard bogie bearings to slide vertically on as the tank rolled over bumps. The crude detail on the hull side had first to be removed to make room for these guides. Above the guides is the upper attachment point for one of the bogies, which will also be removed and replaced with a scratch-built item of better appearance.

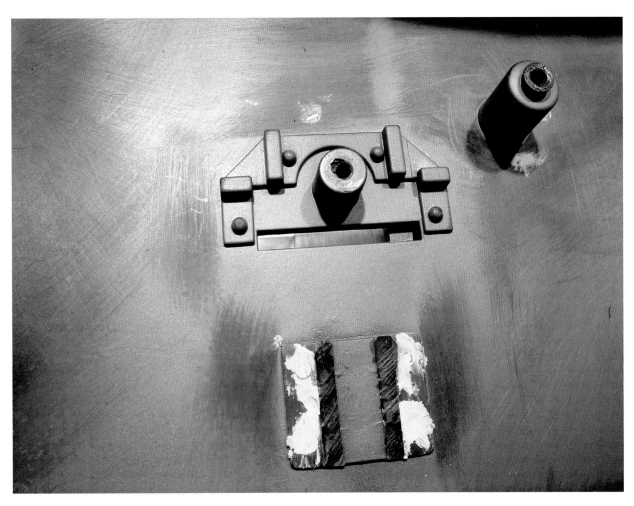

The overly thick detail on the hull side being ground away prior to replacing it.

Two vertical pieces of brass angle which are guides for the inboard bogie bearings to slide vertically on were made from brass angle. These were later replaced with more accurate ones cut from Plastruct H-girder which were shaped and milled.

The guides were initially made from brass angle strips bolted to the hull, since I thought I'd need the strength of metal here even though I wasn't entirely satisfied with their appearance. To the left of the brass strips is one of the lower bogie attachment points which would be ground down and rebuilt. To the right is a slot remaining where the upper bogie attachment seen in photo 021 has been ground off and sanded smooth. Later I would decide that styrene vertical guides would have enough strength and I'd replace these brass guides with better appearing ones made from Plastruct™ 3/8" H-girder. This is described further on in this chapter.

Stage 3 - The Bogies

All eight bogie wheel axle holes were bored out on the lathe to accept a sleeve of 7/16" K & S brass tubing. This acts as a bearing, and will ride on 15/32" brass tubing axles attached to the bogie frame arms. With a moderate amount of lube these bearings will last the life of this radio-controlled model and are much more durable than the original plastic wheels riding on plastic axles, a source of early wear according to many users of the 21st Century Toys Stuart tank.

The tires on the bogie wheels came with an unauthentic square cross-section. Using my Sherline lathe, I rotated the headstock 15 degrees for a taper turning operation. This allows uniform cutting of each bogie's tire to a tapered cross-section which is more realistic.

The tires on the bogie wheels came with an unauthentic square cross-section. Using the Sherline lathe, I rotated the headstock 15 degrees for an operation that is known as taper turning. This allows uniform tapering of each bogie's tire to a tapered cross-section which is more realistic.

The early spoked wheels being converted to the late-war style of solid stamped disk wheels. The wheel on the left is untouched, the center one has four raised spoke ribs milled away, and the wheel on the right has the Panzerwerk resin-cast late-war stamped disk installed. Note the brass bearing sleeve installed in the hubs during a previous operation.

The early spoked wheels were converted to the late-war style of solid stamped disk wheels. This involved using a Dremel tool with an end mill cutter to remove the raised portion of all the bogie wheel spokes. Removing this material allows the resin-cast Panzerwerk™ stamped disk wheels to slide in place. A bench sander was used to remove some material from the back of each disk until a perfect fit was achieved. This occurs when the five raised portions of the disk are flush with the edge of the rim. The outboard and inboard sides of each bogie wheel have different depths, the outboard being shallower. It's only necessary to grind the back faces of the disks intended for the shallow outboard side; the disks going on the deeper inboard side fit just fine as they are.

The unauthentic slot around the periphery of each bogie wheel tire is there for the inaccurate track center guide teeth and had to be eliminated. These gaps were filled in with styrene strips 18" long by .100" wide. These were anchored on each end with a brass brad inserted in a drilled hole. This kept the strip tightly wound inside the slot, and it was further secured with cyanoacrylate glue as it was wound on. This filled the slot about 75%, and Milliput putty was used to complete the filling-in process. Styrene strip is less expensive than Milliput, so I used this means of conserving the use of epoxy putty.

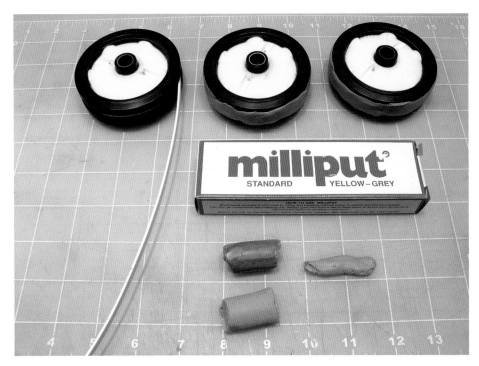

The unauthentic slot around the periphery of each bogie wheel tire was filled in with styrene strip which was anchored on each end with a brass brad. This filled the slot about 75%, and Milliput putty was then used to complete the filling.

The finished bogie wheel with Lion Roar photoetch letters. These were used to make the markings on the tires, both outboard and inboard. The grease nipple and cap fittings may be seen, along with the six rivets equally spaced around the inside of the rim.

Each Panzerwerk wheel disk had two molded-on nipple-type grease fittings when there should have been only one nipple-type and one hex-shaped capped fitting per wheel disk. All 32 of these fittings were ground off and replaced with scratch-built items. It's often easier to make new items than clean up and modify existing ones. Two sizes of styrene disks were punched out using the Waldron Punch & Die set to create both types of fittings: a .120" diameter disk .030" thick and a .081" diameter disk .010" thick. These were glued–the smaller on top of the larger–to the fitting seat on the wheel disk. A .033" hole was drilled down through the two disks to accept a .033" brass rod on which was mounted a 2mm metal bead for the nipple fittings. Plastic nut, bolt, and washer units from Detail Associates™ were used for the grease overflow hex-shaped capped fittings. The raised letters and numbers on the tires were made up from the Lion Roar photoetch sheets. These were placed on the inboard and outboard sides of the tires and read "U.S. TIRE", "MILITARY", and "20 x 6 x 16". Testors liquid cement was used to temporarily attach the brass numbers and letters to the sides of the plastic tires and when dry, a light coat of Super Thin Zap® CA™ glue from Pacer Technology® was applied to anchor them permanently. When dry, the letters were lightly cleaned up with a fine grit sanding stick to round off their square edges. It was somewhat tedious attaching these 368 photoetch pieces, but the results made it worthwhile.

The unauthentic coil springs in the bogies had to be replaced with proper vertical volute springs. It required a fair amount of head scratching and thought before I hit on a way to make them. I used brass strips from K & S Engineering which were .064" thick by 3/4" wide by 18" long. I bought 36" lengths and cut these into two halves 18" long to make the springs. These actually work like the originals did. First, a winding tool or mandrel had to be made. I used a solid brass rod 3/8" in diameter and cut a slot 3/4" deep on one end with a hack saw while the rod was held in a vise. Bending the rod 90 degrees made a good handle for the winding operation.

Brass strip was used to make the vertical volute springs. These actually work like the originals. First, a winding tool or mandrel must be made. Bending the rod 90 degrees makes a good handle for the winding operation.

To make a vertical volute spring, one end of the brass strip is inserted in the slot in the brass rod with its end flush with the slot. To make a uniform and concentric coil the brass strip and winding tool are inserted into the padded nylon jaws of the Panavise. Turning the tool and strip results in a coiled spring.

To make a vertical volute spring, one end of the brass strip was inserted in the slot in the brass rod. A neater coil results if you ensure the end of the strip does not protrude beyond the slot on the other side. This unit was now placed between the hard nylon jaws of my Panavise® and I started turning. These padded jaws will not mar or scratch the brass, as they apply uniform pressure to both sides of the coil as you wind. As the coil increased in diameter I opened up the vise jaws enough so they provided a snug grip on the coil without being so tight that I couldn't turn the coil. As the winding tool became difficult to turn I'd open up the jaws a bit more to produce a looser coil. Don't try to wind the coils too tightly. A properly coiled spring will compress and release without the concentric coils touching each other. This is a desirable condition which will prevent the coils from scratching and rubbing the paint off each other as they compress and expand.

A very nice uniform and concentric coiled vertical volute spring results. After the spring was coiled, the top and bottom of each one was applied to the disk sander to square these ends up–making the ends perpendicular to the long axis of the spring–so they'd fit properly into the mounts I'd make later. Later on in the project I found the weight of the tank to be so great that these vertical volute springs would partially compress, giving the suspension a sagging appearance. The easy fix was to cut sections from coil springs obtained from the hardware store and add them inside the volute springs. They'd be fully enclosed and hidden from view, but they would assist in stiffening up the suspension. I tried several different types of coil springs of varying stiffness before I found the right type and length to use. These coil spring sections would also be added inside the horizontal volute springs for the idler wheels to stiffen them up as well. Once this was done the tank sat at the proper height on its suspension for a fully-loaded M5A1, yet the suspension was not so stiff that it wouldn't articulate as the tank drove over uneven ground. This worked well; sometimes you just get lucky through no fault of your own.

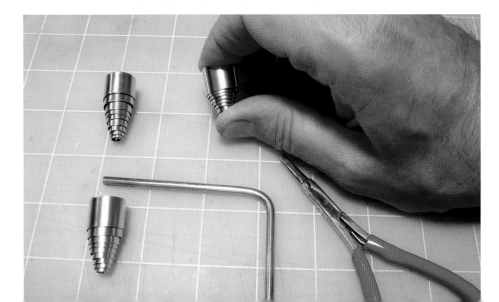

Several vertical volute springs are shown here. At the top left is a finished spring which is fully extended. At the top right I'm compressing another spring to show its range of travel. At the bottom is a spring which needs its top and bottom edges squared up on the disk sander.

The bogie lower arms which support the wheels needed to have recessed areas cut in around the suspension links and axle bolt heads. To ensure all sixteen arms had identical recessed areas, a template was made of .010" sheet styrene and the outlines of the areas were drawn in with a draftsman's pencil.

The lower bogie arms needed recesses cut into them in the area of the attachment for the suspension links and axle bolt heads. To ensure all sixteen bogie arms had identical recesses, a template was made of .010" sheet styrene and the areas to be milled out were drawn on with a draftsman's pencil. The template can be flipped over and used for both right and left bogie arms.

Using an end mill cutter in a Dremel Moto-tool–which was held in a Dremel drill press–all sixteen lower bogie arms had the recesses milled in, about .025" deep. These were then sanded out with a sanding stick.

To do the actual cutting, an end mill cutter was used in my Dremel Moto-tool which was held in the Dremel drill press. A jeweler's anvil provided a flat and level surface to support the bogie lower arms during the milling operation which ensured an even depth of cut.

Several of the bogie lower arms are shown after the milling operation was completed. A sanding stick with four different grits was used to sand out the milled recesses to produce a finished surface.

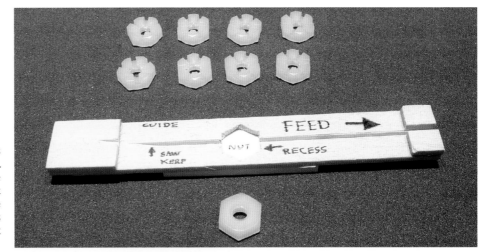

This wooden jig is used to hold the nylon nuts during the process of cutting in their castellations. The jig is run through the micro table saw once to make the first cut, the nut is turned one flat (60°), and this process is repeated two more times. The nut at the bottom of the photo has yet to be run through the saw, while the eight at the top are done.

A step-by-step pictorial view of the cotter pin-making process. On the left is a castellated nut with a length of threaded rod cut off a matching nylon hex-head bolt. The second nut has a .033" hole drilled through the threaded rod in line with one castellation. Above it may be seen a length of brass strip used to make the cotter pins. The third nut shows the bent-up cotter pin ready for insertion. The fourth nut shows the cotter pin in place, and the fifth nut shows the cotter pin legs bent into the safety lock position. The nut is then glued onto one of the inside bogie arms.

Eight nylon nuts situated on the inside surface of the inboard lower bogie arms were converted from plain nuts to castellated ones. A wooden jig was used to hold the nylon nuts during the process of cutting in their castellations. The jig was run through the Preac table saw once to make the first cut, the nut was turned one flat (60°), and this process was repeated two more times. Cotter pins bent up from Detail Associates .015" x .024" brass strip were inserted in holes drilled in the bolts and bent over to a locking position. The brass becomes much more malleable and less springy if you anneal it before bending it to shape. This is easily done by passing the strip through the tip of a candle flame to heat it up, then allowing it to cool. The cotter pins were easily bent to shape using round nose pliers. An alternative is to bend the brass strip around the shank of a sewing needle and pinching the legs of the cotter pin tightly together with square-jaw pliers.

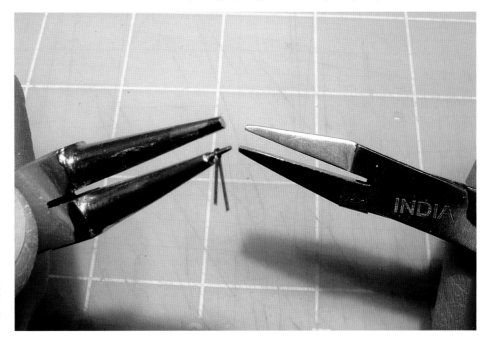

The making of a cotter pin. Brass strip is bent around a mandrel, in this case round-jawed micro pliers, and the eye is then pinched in place with square-jaw pliers.

A Preac Micro-precision miniature table saw makes short work of cutting thick sheets of styrene. It's important to use a rheostat made for power tools which will slow the saw's rpm down so the styrene won't melt from the heat of the saw blade. I use a Dremel Model 217-1 which is foot-operated, placed on the floor, and is very convenient to use.

Using the Preac Micro-Precision miniature table saw made cutting out large and thick pieces of sheet styrene easy, but it was necessary to plug it into a foot-operated rheostat (speed-controlling unit) and slow down the rpm to avoid melting the plastic.

The four bogie frames were extensively modified, almost to the point of having to scratch-build them. They were first partially sawn through in two horizontal places in order to bend them into a sort of Z-angle. As supplied in the kit, their outside plates were straight from top to bottom when they should actually be straight (parallel to the hull) for about one-third the distance down from the top, then flare inboard towards the hull for the second third of their length, then run straight for their bottom third. After this was done a sheet of .020" styrene was used to cover the unauthentic openings on their inboard faces. The bogie frames' unauthentic screw attachments to the hull were cut off and replaced with new mounting flanges built up with various thicknesses of sheet styrene. Structural details and hardware were added to the underside of the top plate, including cutting out the recesses for the vertical volute springs to conform to photos. The sides of the frames were built out with laminations of .080" sheet styrene, and then structural ribs on top of the frames were added from strip styrene.

The bogie end plate showing modifications. It has the correct angled "bent knee" appearance rather than being a straight flat plate.

The four bogie frames after texturing with Mr. Surfacer 500 and adding all the brass hardware.

The bogie frames have track skids made from .030" thick brass strip. These protected the bogies from track slap when the tank was traversing rough terrain. They were sawn from brass strip on the table saw to a width of 3/8" and formed using round-nose pliers and bending around solid brass rod used as a mandrel. The two spring plugs in the top are 3/16" set screws, while the two vertical guides for the spider link axle bearings were cut from a Plastruct 3/8" H-column and fashioned into "T" shapes. All of the incorrect round bolt heads were cut off and replaced with brass nuts, bolts, and washers inserted into drilled and tapped holes.

The bogie frames were given a stippled coat of Mr. Surfacer prior to the attachment of all the hardware to replicate the cast foundry texture. Now they're beginning to look more like the real thing.

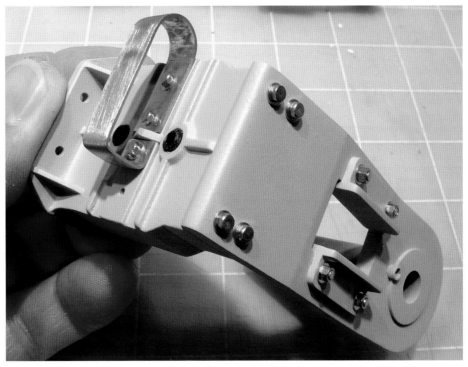

Each bogie frame has a track skid made from .030" thick brass strip. These were sawn on the table saw to a width of 3/8" and formed using round-nose pliers and bending around solid brass rod. The two spring plugs in the top are 3/16" set screws, while the two vertical guides were cut from Plastruct 3/8" H-column and fashioned into "T" shapes.

The four bogie spider links had to be scratch-built to replace the toy-like kit ones. Sheet styrene .120" thick was cut into strips, then into short sections to make up these links.

The bogie spider links were scratch-built to replace the kit's toy-like ones, which bore only a passing resemblance to the originals. Strip styrene .120" thick was sawn into strips on the table saw. These were then cut into short sections to make up the links. A construction jig was used to ensure the links were identical to each other. Brass pins were used to reinforce the joints of four end pieces of the spider links.

The shape and profile of the spider links were built up with strip and sheet styrene, and Milliput putty was used for blending and filling. Eight steps in making a spider link half are shown.

An assembly jig was fashioned from .080" sheet styrene which ensured all eight sections of the spider links would be identical. Number #1 is in the jig, and the progress of each one runs through number #8.

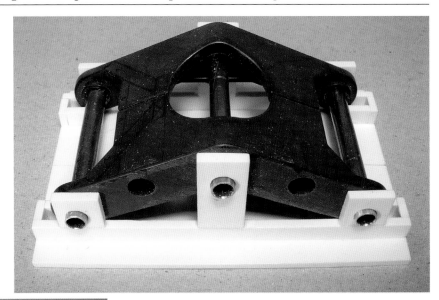

The assembly jig was modified with six vertical lugs made of .080" sheet styrene to adapt it into a hole-drilling jig. The kit's inaccurate spider link was used as a template to locate the positions of the six holes to be drilled. Once done, this jig was used to locate the six holes drilled into each of the four scratch-built spider links so each would be identical.

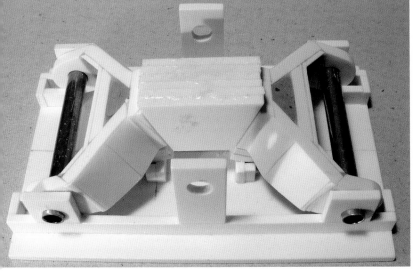

The assembly jig was then modified to include six uprights with holes (using the kit's unauthentic spider link as a template) which would be used to accurately drill the lift link holes in the spider links.

A wedge-shaped center section was made up as a lamination of six pieces of .080" sheet styrene and glued to two spider link halves to complete the unit. Foundry casting numbers were added from the Lion Roar photoetch numbers sheets. When finished the spider links were given a rough-cast foundry texture by stippling on a coat of Mr. Surfacer 500.

Above: Two halves of the spider link were located in the jig, then they were joined by a wedge-shaped center section made up of six laminated pieces of .080" sheet styrene.

Right: The four spider links finished and textured with Mr. Surfacer 500 which was stippled on with an old brush. Note the foundry casting numbers made from Lion Roar photoetch numbers.

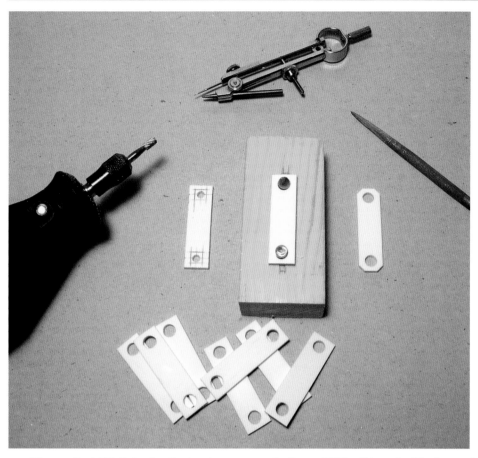

The vertical bogie links were made from .080" sheet styrene. A jig was made of a block of wood with two short lengths of 3/16" brass rod, and this was used to ensure the proper spacing of the drilled holes in both ends of the links.

The vertical lift links for the bogies were made from .080" sheet styrene. A jig was made of a block of wood with two short lengths of 3/16" brass rod, which was used to ensure the proper spacing of the drilled holes in both ends of the links, a necessary mass-production method when making the 32 links.

Stage 4 - The lower hull, Part B
The four axle brackets inboard of the bogies were made from .030" styrene sheet and 1-72 brass bolts and nuts. These replaced the kit's unauthentic half-hex shaped units located on the hull bottom that had no side hull detail and which were ground away.

The four axle brackets were made from .030" styrene sheet and 1-72 brass bolts & nuts.

An inboard view of an axle bracket which replaced the kit's unauthentic half-hex shaped units located on the hull bottom which had no side hull detail and were ground away.

The axle bracket clamps were detailed with a vertical saw cut creating the clamp, along with the tightening bolts and nuts.

The final version of the hull-mounted vertical guides for the spider link axles and bearings was cut from a Plastruct 3/8" H-section girder. I cut out the angled sections on the Preac table saw. Recesses for the attaching nuts were milled in with a cutter chucked into a Dremel tool mounted in a drill stand. These guides were then drilled and bolted on with 1-72 bolts and nuts. After finishing them they had a much better appearance than the initial ones I made from brass angle and are just as strong once bolted in place. There are 40 pieces in these details.

Two of the eight bogie guides which were cut from Plastruct H-girder, then shaped. Recesses for the wrench to tighten the nuts were milled out using a cutter in a Dremel mounted on a drill stand.

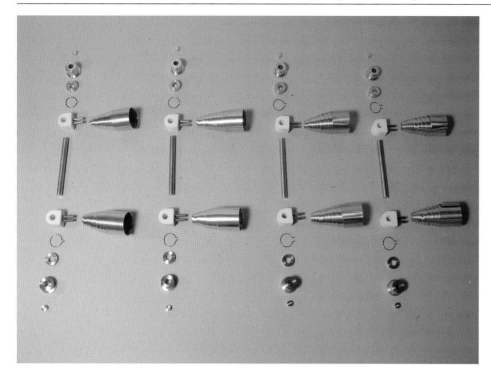

A lineup of the scratch-built suspension parts for the four bogies. The Sherline lathe proved indispensable for making these types of parts. The eight snap rings were made from annealed brass rod.

Stage 5 - Final comments on the bogies

Many of the bogie components needed for articulation were turned on the lathe, including the spider link axle; the bearings and caps, which slide vertically in the bogie frame and hull guides; and spacers. Other hardware was fashioned, including snap rings made of .028" brass wire. The eight vertical volute spring plugs or mounts were built up as a block of laminated .080" sheet styrene, shaped, then each was drilled for two 1/16" brass tubing retaining pins for the volute springs.

The bogies, with all their pieces, needed frequent dry-fitting and adjustment during fabrication and assembly. Having to make scale components in this size was a new experience for me, but the additional complexity of having to make them operational in addition to creating a scale appearance was often a challenge. I found my eyes becoming crossed as I pondered these challenges late into the night on frequent occasions.

One of the assembled bogies after final fit adjustment and prior to painting. The brass vertical volute springs allow the bogie to function exactly as the original did.

Side view of the unpainted bogie showing all the varied materials making up its construction.

Despite having to often modify, redo, replace, and otherwise adjust parts to allow scale appearance *and* operation, there came a great feeling of satisfaction at having eventually done it. Watching it all articulate precisely and in a scale manner made all the challenges worthwhile.

The finished bogies are a major change from the kit-supplied ones, both in appearance and operation.

Profile of painted bogie wheel assembly.

Comparison of rebuilt bogie to kit bogie.

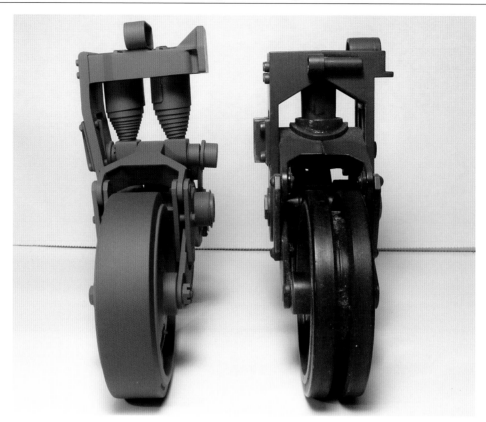

End view of rebuilt bogie and kit bogie. Note slots in wheels which have been filled. The top of the rebuilt bogie is not quite square due to the pressure of the springs. This will disappear when the bogies are bolted up to the hull.

The bogies are about 85% scratch-built and add authenticity to the model.

Three-quarter view of finished bogie.

The bogie temporarily attached to the hull. Everything articulates, slides, and moves as per the original.

When temporarily attached to the hull, it was fascinating to watch the bogie articulate precisely as the original did, and to see the center bearing caps slide up and down within the vertical guides in both the bogie and on the hull.

Another view of the bogie showing the central spider link attached to eight lift links. There is a brass shaft running through the spider link, through the spring plugs, and into the bearing caps which fit into the vertical guides on the bogie and on the hull. These bearing caps slide up and down within the guides as the tank moves over uneven ground and this motion is dampened by the vertical volute springs.

The sprocket final drive housing textured with Mr. Surfacer 500 and with all the brass bolts safety lock wired.

Stage 6 - Finishing up the final drive units

At this point the final drive units were textured with Mr. Surfacer 500. The final drive units were then primered and painted. Safety lock wire taken from electrical wire strands was run through the drilled-out bolt heads.

Stage 7 - The return rollers

The return rollers needed modification to enhance their appearance and to allow the track guide teeth to clear their mounting shafts. This involved cutting off the plastic collars of the rollers, lathing off their indistinct round-headed bolts on their hubs, and scratch-building everything else. Brass tubing was used for bearings inside the plastic parts, while solid brass rod was used for both the mounting shafts and mounting plates.

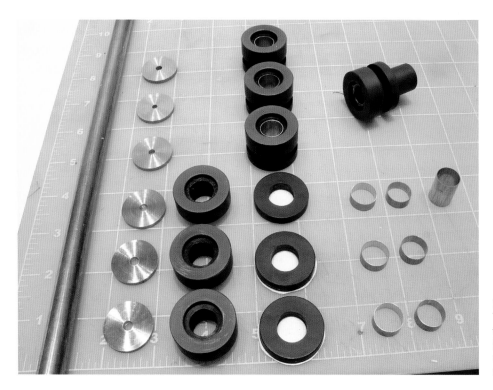

Modifying the six track support or return rollers. This involved filling the center slots, adding brass tubing bearings, creating new mounts, adding hardware, and other details. One of the kit's original return rollers may be seen at the upper right.

Preparing to mill out the return roller shafts for track guide teeth clearance. The Sherline lathe set up with a vertical milling table and a milling vise.

For the milling of the return roller shafts a Sherline vertical milling table accessory was set up on the lathe and a milling vise was used to hold the parts to be machined absolutely rigid.

Using a collet to hold the cutting tool yields a more precise and accurately centered cut than the standard three-jaw chuck. A milling vise holds the part much more securely than a standard vise, essential for milling operations, where there is more vibration and heavier side loads than when lathing.

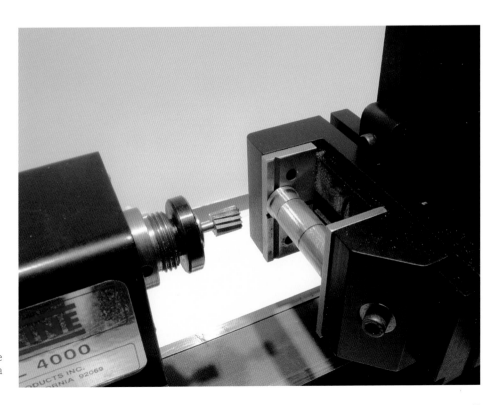

Chucking a cutting tool into a collet will make a more precise and accurate cut than using a regular chuck.

The actual milling operation is very precise and easy. It's a good idea to wear eye protection and use a respirator mask since the milled-out brass particles are very small and light and can be inhaled.

The actual milling operation is easy and precise. It's a good idea to wear eye protection and use a respirator mask since the milled out brass particles are very light and can be inhaled.

The milled-out recess was brought to its final profile with .030" sheet styrene and Milliput, and the excess was carved and sanded away when dry, resulting in a nice circular fillet.

The final milled-out slot is brought to its final contour with .030" sheet styrene and Milliput. The brass-tubing socket in the return roller can be seen.

A triangular gusset made from .030" brass strip reinforces the roller shaft at the bottom. This view shows the track end connector teeth riding smoothly forward through the milled-out recess.

A triangular reinforcing gusset made from .030" brass strip was added to the bottoms of the return roller shafts. The necessity for the milled-out recesses is apparent in the view of the track end connectors' guide teeth sailing unimpeded through the milled-out area on their way forward to the drive sprockets.

Six hub caps were made from .040" sheet styrene, and each has six plastic bolt heads sliced from Plastruct 1/16" hex rod which were drilled and safety-wired. The five brass 2-56 bolts securing each return roller shaft mounting plate to the hull were also drilled out and safety-wired.

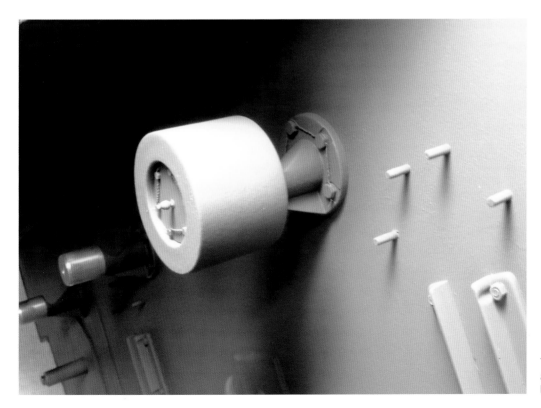

The finished return roller in place with a hub cap, bolts, and safety wire on both the cap and mount.

A comparison of the idler wheels before and after extensive modifications.

Stage 8 - The idler wheels, arms, and brackets

The two idler wheels were given extensive modifications. The spokes were re-contoured to a continuous concave curve, and the unauthentic inner "box" structure enclosing the groove around the circumference of the wheels was milled away on both sides and the resulting openings were filled with .060" sheet styrene. An inner plate made from .020" sheet styrene was added in each of the 7 spoke bays around the inner circumference of the wheels on both sides. Grease fittings were made from sheet styrene and brass rod, and the rubber tires were strips cut from .120" sheet styrene which covered up the unauthentic slots around the circumference of the wheels designed to accommodate the unauthentic track center guides. The tires have brass photo-etched numbers and letters from Lion Roar which make up the "30 x 8 x 26" and "MILITARY" and "FIRESTONE" raised markings. Milliput epoxy putty was used to make the weld beads in all 28 spoke bays.

Two bearing sleeves were cut from brass tubing to decrease rolling friction, and the unauthentic idler axles were used to lathe end caps which retain the bearing sleeves in place.

The idler wheels with their new tires and photoetch markings. Brass tubing was used to make inner and outer bearing sleeves to decrease rolling friction, and the old styrene axles were lathed down to make retaining caps, seen here in Olive Drab.

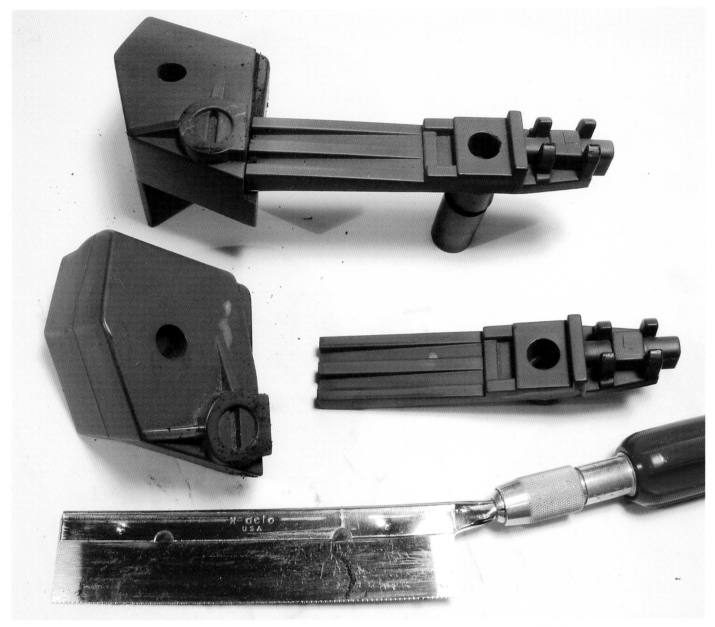

The idler arms were sawn off the volute spring brackets in the first step of extensive modifications.

The idler arms and volute spring brackets were inaccurate in shape with simplified detail. Both needed extensive modifications. As the kit is designed there is only one idler arm on each side of the hull. This is solidly attached to the idler bracket. The entire idler bracket pivots with the single arm as the tank traverses rough terrain, the idler wheel's inboard portion of the axle riding up and down in a spring-dampened channel in the side of the hull. This is not very authentic in appearance or operation. The first step to fix this state of affairs was to acquire a second set of left and right idler bracket/arm pieces from a seller on an online auction who was "parting out" his Stuart tank. Once these pieces arrived, the second step was to separate the four arms from the brackets with an X-ACTO razor saw.

Because the resin tracks would be dimensionally different from the kit's tracks, and because they would loosen up and lengthen with use, an authentic operating track tensioning system had to be made. The arms had rectangular openings cut in to accommodate a threaded rod axle and two sliding guide blocks cut from square brass tubing. The teeth on the adjustment rack were made with .040" triangular styrene strip. This was duplicated on the inside face of the scratch-built adjustment plates which have a threaded rod, washer, and adjusting nut added. The idler arms were further modified with the proper size strengthening ribs cut from styrene sheet which replaced the oversize ones that were cut and sanded away. The horns at the end of the idler arm which retain the adjusting nut in place were reshaped and rebuilt with styrene sheet. Hexagonal nylon nuts were run through the table saw in a jig to cut slots into one face, making them into castellated nuts. Cotter pins will be made from brass strip and added later.

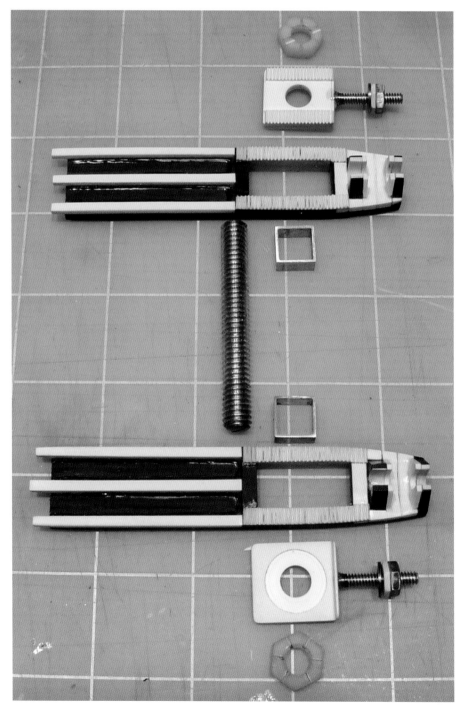

Some of the parts made and modifications done to allow realistic and authentic operation of the idler wheel and track tensioning system.

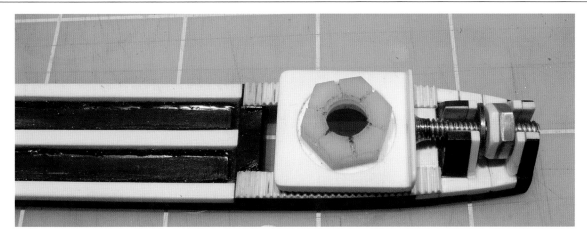

The track tensioning system in a close-up view: the track tool which appears as a double ended wrench stowed on the tank's engine deck fits both sizes of nuts seen here and is actually used to adjust the track tension.

The track tensioning tool stowed on the aft hull plate of the tank has an open-end wrench on one end and a box wrench on the other. These two wrench sizes fit both nuts seen in the photos, and the tool is actually used to make adjustments to the track tension on the model, just as in the full-size tank. The idler arm strengthening ribs shown in white have several applications of white glue where they join the arm as a fillet to represent the curves seen in the original foundry casting. These will smooth up after texturing with Mr. Surfacer 500 and the application of primer and top coats of paint. Foundry casting numbers from the Lion Roar brass photoetch sheets were added to the four guide plates.

The track tensioning system in place to check fit, alignment, and operation. Foundry casting numbers from the Lion Roar brass photoetch sheets were added to the guide plates.

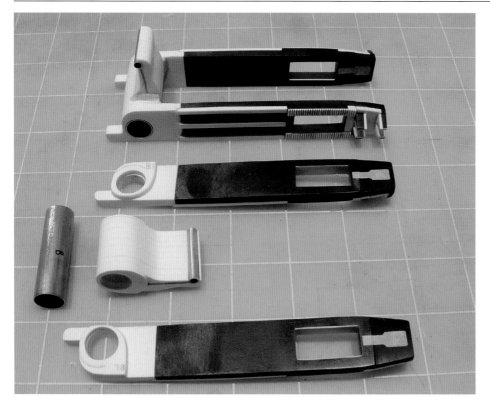

The scratch-built components of the idler arm assembly at the front, with an assembled idler arm at the rear.

The forward ends of the idler arms and the vertical cam portion of the arm which rides against the volute spring were laminated up from .80" sheet styrene and shaped with an end mill cutter. Weld lines were made from thin rolled lengths of Milliput. Brass tubing was used for a bearing for the idler arms to pivot on, and also to represent the anti-wear tube on the face of the cam.

The idler wheel bracket had to be extensively reshaped and modified, necessary not only for accuracy, but also to allow the entire mechanism to have an operating spring action as per the original. The bracket was cut apart and a proper size plastic pill bottle was grafted onto it. The bracket was reshaped using sheet styrene and Zap CA medium viscosity glue to bring it to a correct appearance. Unauthentic holes were filled, cast depressions were created, and fillets were made of .040" sheet styrene.

The first three stages of modifying the idler spring brackets: the kit's bracket, the cut open bracket with a pill bottle grafted onto it, and creating more authentic shapes and contours.

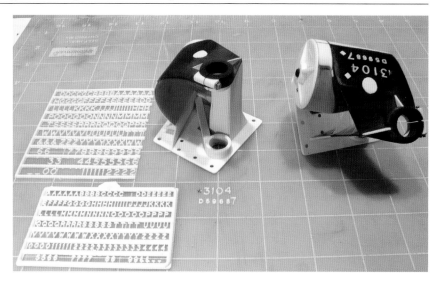

The idler bracket with more details, including foundry casting numbers and letters in two sizes from Kit Kraft.

Internal and external details were added from brass, sheet and strip styrene, and Allen set screws. Foundry casting numbers and letters came from styrene letters molded by Kit Kraft™. The idler arm pivots on a brass tubing shaft which causes the horn to push against the spring seat, compressing the horizontal volute spring. The volute spring was made from K & S ¾" x .015" brass strip wound on a mandrel. The track skid on top of the bracket was bent up from 3/8" x .060" brass strip.

A view of the various parts and components making up the left rear idler wheel, bracket, and operating horizontal volute spring system. The volute spring was made of K & S ¾" x .015" brass strip wound on a mandrel.

A close-up of the idler bracket showing details. The track skid on top was made up of K & S 3/8" x .060" brass strip.

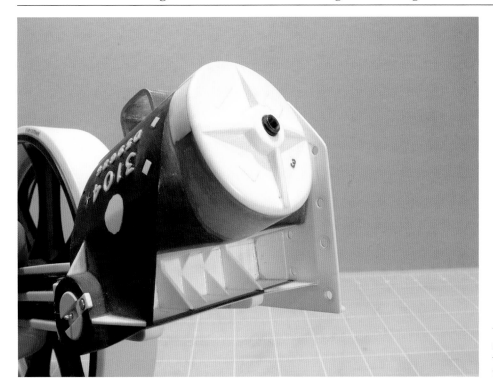

The front of the idler bracket shows the inset area with gussets made of .040" sheet styrene. In the front center is a 3/16" socket head set screw from the hardware store.

The front of the bracket has a 3/16" socket head set screw from the hardware store screwed in, and has an inset area boxed in with .040 sheet styrene with gussets made of the same material. Various weld seams were made of Milliput putty and stretched sprue. The idler arm has two horn extensions on its forward edge which act as stops to prevent the arm from swinging below a level position.

The idler arm horn was laminated up from .080" sheet styrene. When the idler wheel is deflected up by terrain, this horn pushes forward against the spring seat (a disk laminated up from .125" and .040" sheet styrene) which then compresses the spring.

The underside of the bracket shows the two horns which act as stops to prevent the idler arm from swinging down below a level position. The weld lines were made from Milliput.

The entire idler wheel, arm, and bracket assembly is large and took a fair amount of time to construct, but this complex assembly looks and operates like the real thing. Well worth the effort. Most of the pieces will be textured with Gunze Sangyo Mr. Surfacer 500 to represent a rough foundry cast finish.

The size of the idler wheel and bracket assembly can be seen by comparing it to a hand. This is a large model and will take some time to finish.

6

The Air Deflectors

Scratch-building the lower air deflectors

The air deflectors turned the hot air coming vertically down from the engine cooling air outlet at the rear of the hull overhang and turned it 90 degrees to exit straight aft. This reduced the amount of the dust cloud the real tank raised, making it much less visible in combat. These deflectors were fitted to the Stuart some time after its introduction to combat when the requirement for them became very evident.

The two lower rear air deflectors were made from sheet brass using .015" for the side plates and .010" for the main housing and two interior vanes. These were soldered up with silver solder. Other stiffeners and flanges inside were made from .010" styrene sheet and strip.

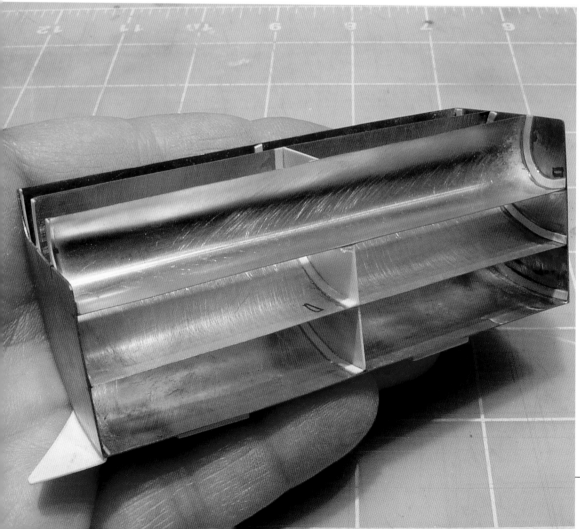

One of the two lower air deflectors made from brass sheet, and sheet styrene and strip.

AMACO copper wire mesh was used for the expanded steel screening covering the air deflector outlets. The larger size is 1/4", and the smaller is 1/8".

The expanded steel mesh covering the deflector outlets was made from AMACO® copper mesh in 1/4" and 1/8" sizes obtained from an art supply store. These two sizes of mesh exactly duplicate the weave and size of the openings of the actual screens in 1/6 scale, a curious and serendipitous affair which makes you scratch your head and wonder how you got so lucky. The deflectors have mounting straps made from .010" brass sheet, and 2-56 bolts hold them to the aft hull plate. Four mounting pads were made from .100" x .180" styrene strip and were detailed with Milliput weld beads. Eight 0-80 bolts hold S-plates made from .010" brass sheet to these four pads. These assemblies acted as clamps to hold canvas covers in place. These were used with the pre-heater when it was hooked up to warm the engines in cold weather.

Scratch-building the upper air deflector
The upper air deflector is described here in this chapter along with the lower air deflector for continuity, although it was actually built much later in the project; that is, after the hull was completed and the turret was mounted. This seemed the most logical time to make

and mount it, since it had to be constructed to fit after the hull was completed. It also reduced the chance of accidental damage to the deflector since it was to be installed towards the end of the project.

The one-piece upper air deflector was made in the same manner as the lower two, but has additional parts, since on the actual vehicle it had to unlatch, swivel upwards towards the front, and latch in that raised position to clear the four engine access doors behind it when it was necessary to open them for engine maintenance.

The hull mounts were made from brass plate, the deflector arms from .015" sheet, the hinge pins from brass rod, and the cotter pins from brass strip. The strap and hinge on the bottom of the deflector secure it in the down position by bolting to the second engine door and are made from .015" brass sheet and rod. A 2-56 hex-head bolt and washer secure the strap.

The deflector was given some dents and minor bending to portray damage suffered while in combat to conform to period photographs which depict this. The upper air deflector is illustrated later on in the book.

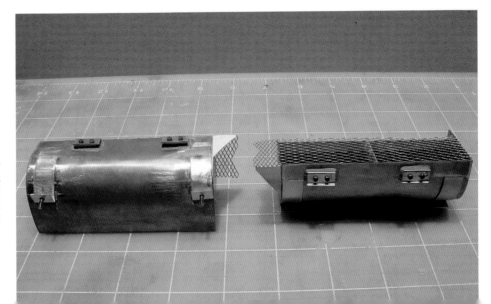

Details on the underside of the lower air deflectors include mounting straps and bolts. Four pads with Milliput weld beads were added which are the mounting points for the eight bolts holding four S-plates in place. These plates held the engine pre-heater covers in place.

7

Finishing the Lower Hull

Painting schedule outline

1. Textured with Gunze Sangyo Mr. Surfacer 500.
2. Airbrushed Floquil® Reefer Gray primer.
3. Airbrushed Floquil Olive Drab base coat.
4. Airbrushed a post-shading of Floquil dark Olive Drab.
5. Airbrushed Floquil light Olive Drab highlighting in center of panels.
6. Airbrushed markings with Floquil Reefer White and Reefer Yellow using stencils.
7. Applied a pin wash of Burnt Umber oil color to recesses and around all raised details.
8. Applied three filters with a brush using Raw Sienna oil paint.
9. Airbrushed Floquil Mud & Dust to suspension, along sides, and lightly on top.
10. Airbrushed Testors Dullcote™ overall.
11. Applied powdered graphite to edges and all metallic equipment.
12. Weathered with Doc O'Brien's™ Weathering Powders.

Painting schedule in detail

1. Gunze Sangyo Mr. Surfacer 500 was stippled on to give the cast surfaces of the tank the rough-cast texture of the original foundry parts. Stippling is a technique where the artist wields the brush using sharp jabs to apply the paint rather than brushing it on. I used a 1/4" wide flat brush that had its bristles clipped short to 1/4 inch in length to produce a firmer brush for this. It was necessary to clean the brush frequently since Mr. Surfacer is a liquid putty which builds up on the brush quickly. Stippling can be a tedious and lengthy process since the model is so big, but listening to music during this task makes it less onerous and the job seems to go faster.

2. The hull was airbrushed with a primer coat of Floquil Reefer Gray. This primer coat reveals any flaws in workmanship which you will want to correct before the final finish is applied. It also gives the model a monochromatic finish that nicely covers the dissimilar plastic, brass, resin, and white metal components of the model and gives them a uniform density and reflectance. This simplifies the application of the finish coats of the Olive Drab base coat.

3. When the primer had cured for several days, Olive Drab was then airbrushed as a base coat. This was mixed up from Floquil Roof Brown (18 units), Depot Olive (10 units), and Reefer Yellow (3 units). This 18:10:3 ratio produces a very reasonable U.S. Army World War II freshly painted Olive Drab. This color was lightened and darkened for highlighting and shadowing of various components during the weathering stage. The real World War II Olive Drab paint was made by several manufacturers using varying ingredients which weathered differently depending on temperature, humidity, exposure to sunlight, and other factors. This means it would be difficult for an expert to be overly critical of the exact formula you use for your Olive Drab. Moreover, the various weathering techniques used later are going to alter this color even more, so my advice would be to do your best to be reasonably accurate when first mixing it up, and then cease to worry about it.

4. When dry, a darker shade of OD was airbrushed along weld lines, seams, around panel edges, and in recesses. A lighter shade of OD was then used in the center of the various panels to highlight them. This three-shading effect gives the model life, depth, and makes it look more realistic and interesting. The drive sprockets and idler wheels received the three-shading effect as well.

5. A lighter shade of Olive Drab was then lightly airbrushed in the center of certain panels and areas to break up the monochromatic look of a single shade of paint. On a model this large this technique makes it look much more realistic.

6. A detailed step-by-step process for painting the stenciled markings is given in "Working with stencils" in Chapter 12.

7. A pin wash of Burnt Umber oil paint–mixed up at the ratio of 80% thinner to 20% paint–was applied with a fine brush

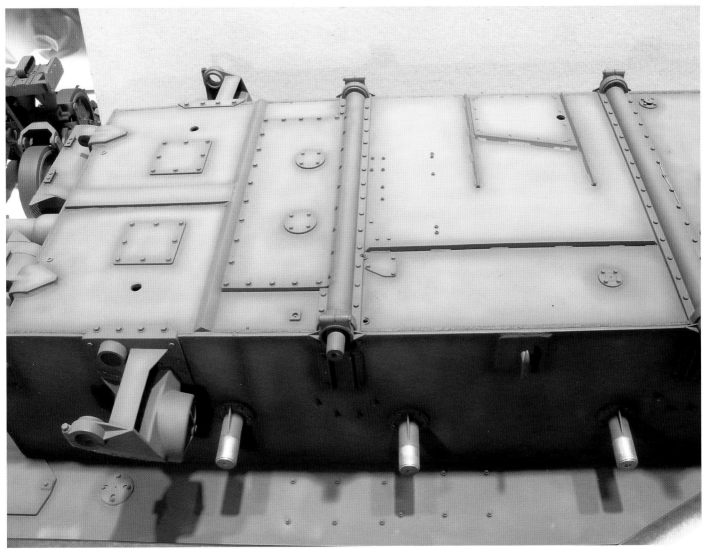

The hull was airbrushed Olive Drab as a base coat. When dry, a darker shade of OD was airbrushed along weld lines, seams, around panel edges, and in recesses. A lighter shade of OD was then used in the center of the various panels as a highlight. This three-shading effect gives the model life, depth, and makes it look more realistic and interesting.

around all recessed and raised detail to create a shadow effect that enhances their visibility.

8. Three filters–or general washes–were mixed up at the ratio of 95% thinner to 5% Raw Sienna oil paint to create a dust effect in layers. These filters were applied to the model overall using a 1/2-inch wide flat brush with special emphasis on areas prone to collect dust, such as the top surfaces of the hull. It's important to use a thinner that will not attack the paint already applied.

9. A much diluted coat (90% thinner, 10% paint) of Floquil Mud was very lightly airbrushed onto the suspension, tracks, and around the lower hull, building this effect up slowly and carefully in areas likely to collect mud. Another thin coat of Floquil Dust was airbrushed on the sides of the hull and turret, taking care to apply this with vertical strokes to appear as rain-streaked weathering. A light veil of Dust was airbrushed on the horizontal surfaces of the turret and hull as well.

10. Testors Dullcote was airbrushed over all surfaces of the model to give it a uniform flat reflectance and to seal the finish coats prior to further weathering.

11. Graphite powder taken from a draftsman's pencil sharpener was gently rubbed along all edges of the model subject to abrasion from crew and brush to indicate paint wear. This was also applied to the machine guns, which gives them a realistic metallic sheen.

12. Doc O'Brien's Weathering Powders (ground pastels) were used to add further weathering to indicate mud, rust, dust, paint wear, and abrasion. These can be applied dry but can wear off with handling. Applying them wet with thinner will make them more permanent, but it's difficult to see their true effect until they're dry, so go lightly with them at first, building up succeeding layers if required.

The drive sprockets and idler wheels received the three-shading effect as well. A silver Prismacolor pencil was used to indicate wear on the sprocket drive teeth.

A Berol® Prismacolor™ Silver 959 pencil was used to indicate wear on the sprocket drive teeth. Using the side of the point to deposit a broad streak of silver, a sponge-tip makeup applicator was used to buff the silver out into a subdued and indistinct wear pattern on the teeth.

Windsor & Newton™ oil colors were used to add subtle weathering, dust, and rust to various parts. These colors were feathered out with a brush using odorless paint thinner, which did not affect the underlying lacquer-base coat of Floquil Olive Drab. The color used most was Burnt Umber, which gives an excellent representation of rust. Oil paints have the quality of easily being blended into their surroundings to give an understated effect.

Windsor & Newton oil colors were used to add subtle weathering, dust, and rust to various parts. These colors were blended out using odorless paint thinner which did not affect the underlying lacquer-base coat of Olive Drab, mixed up from Floquil paints.

The drive sprockets, bogies, and idlers were bolted to the hull, imperfections were touched up, and an overcoat of Testors Dullcote was airbrushed overall to seal the paint.

The drive sprockets, bogies, and idlers were bolted to the hull. The drive sprockets required hub caps to cover the screws attaching them to the final drives, and these were made from .020" sheet styrene with cupped holes drilled in. All imperfections were then touched up, and an overcoat of Testors Dullcote was airbrushed overall to seal the paint.

8

Creating the T16E1 Tracks from Resin Castings

The kit's tracks did not resemble the proper T16E1 tracks the M5A1 carried. They were toy-like and had unauthentic center guides. These tracks had to be replaced somehow. A commercial resin caster (the gentlemanly Rob Ervin of Formations Models™) agreed to take on the project if I made the masters of one track block and one end connector. I made these two parts using styrene, a brass nut and bolt, and photoetch foundry casting numbers. Rob made up over 140 track blocks and 280 end connectors in a gray resin that resembled cast steel. I think having to endlessly cast these hundreds of pieces made Rob a little crazy, and he advised me he would prefer not to have to do this again during his lifetime. I believe I publicly mention his name here at my own risk.

The kit's tracks were toy-like, had unauthentic center guides, did not resemble the T16E1 tracks of the Stuart, but I bet they ran well. They had to be replaced.

Masters of the track block and end connector were made up from styrene, a brass nut and bolt, and photoetch foundry casting numbers. Notice the authentic Floquil Reefer Gray carefully airbrushed onto the fingertips.

A commercial resin caster (Rob Ervin of Formations Models) made up over 132 track blocks and 264 end connectors in a gray resin which resembled cast steel. I'm not certain Rob has recovered yet. These were cleaned up and joined with track pins made of 1/16" K & S brass tubing.

When the resin parts arrived they were cleaned up and joined with track pins made of sections cut from 1/16" K & S brass tubing. An X-ACTO razor saw separated the pour plugs from the parts, then CA glue was used to fill the many pits and pin holes inherent in casting large parts in resin. The track blocks have dimples, cuts, scrapes, and signs of other damage to replicate the appearance of real rubber blocks which have seen much use on hard terrain.

A drilling jig was constructed from balsa wood to hold the end connectors firmly in place and absolutely square to the drill bit so the 1/16" holes for the link pins could be drilled accurately.

A drilling jig was constructed from balsa wood to hold the end connectors firmly in place and square to the drill bit so the 1/16" holes for the link pins could be drilled accurately. Doing this would allow the tracks to run straight and true, with no binding or stress, and have a scale appearance. Sanding sticks, files, and fingernail polishing blocks were used to clean up any rough edges and extra resin flash.

An X-ACTO razor saw separated the pour plugs from the parts, then CA glue was used to fill any pits or pin holes. Sanding sticks, files, and polishing pads were used to clean up rough edges and extra resin flash.

After final assembly the first track was mounted on the tank to check fit and function before painting.

After one track was assembled it was mounted on the tank to check fit and function. Since the drive sprocket teeth had been reconfigured to a major degree for accuracy, it was a relief to see the track mesh nicely with the drive sprocket during running. The track was fitted and tensioned up in the identical manner as the full-size tank using the scale track tensioning tool (wrench). The track ran smoothly around the idler wheel, even during the up-and-down movement of the idler during running over rough ground. The track operated in a smooth and realistic manner around the suspension components while running over obstacles, a delight to see. I felt fortunate this turned out so well, not always the case... sigh. The size of the model is readily apparent when compared to a hand.

The drive sprocket meshed well with the end connectors during running. This was of concern since the profiles of the sprocket teeth had been reconfigured for accuracy.

After tensioning up the track in the exact manner of the full-size vehicle, it ran smoothly around the rear idler wheel, even during the vertical movement of the idler arm suspension.

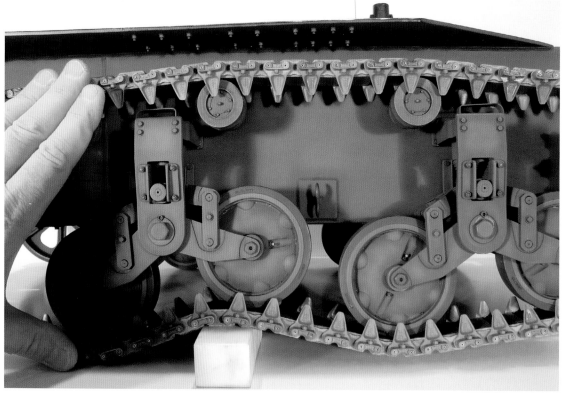

The track ran smoothly during the movement of the suspension components while running over obstacles. The size of the model is apparent when compared to a hand.

Awash in a sea of track blocks and end connectors. Two large sheets of styrofoam were used to hold the track blocks and end connectors for drying after airbrushing and weathering these parts with oil paints.

Two large sheets of styrofoam were used to hold the track blocks and end connectors for drying after these parts were airbrushed, weathered with oil paints, and flat-coated with Testors Dullcote. I used toothpicks (cocktail sticks) as a handle for each piece during the painting and drying process.

9

Wiring Up the Electronics

Before you become intimidated and cross-eyed by the technicalities inherent in this electronics chapter, I hasten to reassure the reader that I had minimal experience with any of this myself before this project was started. I simply went online and conducted searches for the various things I wanted to learn, and in so doing I became self-educated enough that I was able to successfully wire everything up to my satisfaction. Ah, the joys of the Internet! Many thanks to all the electronics experts who took the time to create websites sharing what they know with the rest of us amateurs!

The lighting system is comprised of seven light-emitting diodes (LEDs). Three 5mm ultra-bright whites are for the two headlights and the spotlight, while four 3mm yellows are used for the two blackout driving lights mounted above the headlights and also the two taillights. A piece of styrofoam was used as a base for a "breadboard" set-up to verify and finalize the wiring of the LEDs in this parallel system. A digital multimeter was used to measure the voltage running through the LEDs to make sure it was within proper limits and that the correct value resistors were being used. Too much resistance and the LEDs won't illuminate. Too little and they burn out.

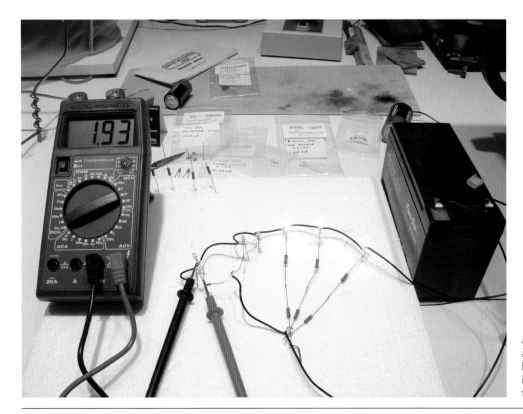

A "breadboard" set-up was used to create and finalize the parallel wiring of the seven LEDs in the lighting system. A multimeter is being used here to verify voltage flowing through a yellow LED is within limits.

M5A1 STUART LIGHTING SYSTEM

Parallel wiring system for 7 LEDs

Three 5mm ultra-bright white LEDs were used for the two headlights and the spotlight. The forward voltage limits for the whites are 3.6~4.0 volts. Actual measured voltage was 3.7~3.9 volts.

Four 3mm yellow LEDs were used for the two blackout driving lights and the two taillights. The forward voltage limits for yellows are 1.7~2.2 volts. Actual measured voltage was 1.93 volts.

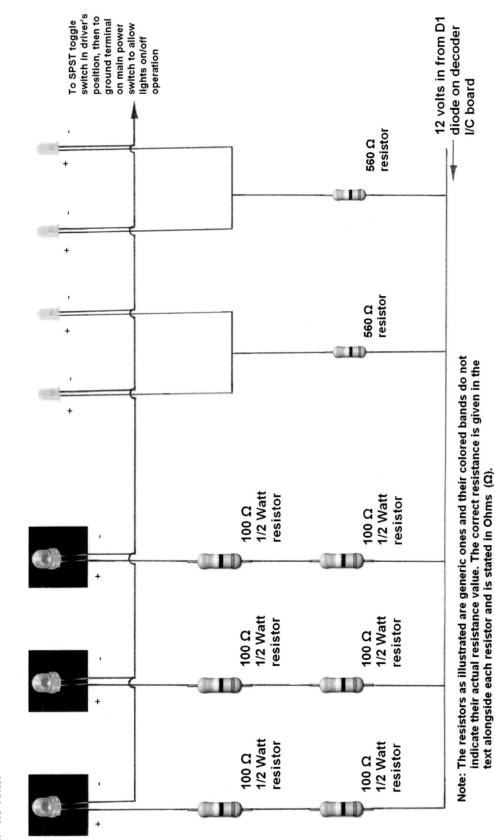

To SPST toggle switch in driver's position, then to ground terminal on main power switch to allow lights on/off operation

12 volts in from D1 diode on decoder I/C board

560 Ω resistor

560 Ω resistor

100 Ω 1/2 Watt resistor

100 Ω 1/2 Watt resistor

100 Ω 1/2 Watt resistor

100 Ω 1/2 Watt resistor

100 Ω 1/2 Watt resistor

100 Ω 1/2 Watt resistor

Note: The resistors as illustrated are generic ones and their colored bands do not indicate their actual resistance value. The correct resistance is given in the text alongside each resistor and is stated in Ohms (Ω).

A pictorial schematic diagram I made up of the lighting system which formalized the breadboard set-up. It shows the wiring and values for all the components used so I can remember all this stuff later on.

An overview of the hull with the electronics and wiring installed. The speaker has been relocated from mid-hull on the floor aft to the engine compartment.

I created a pictorial schematic diagram (*see* p 67) to illustrate the wiring and all the components with their values to help me understand it more clearly, and also as a record of how everything should be wired up. This was helpful much later on when the turret was added; I now had a diagram of how to connect everything back to the hull wiring rather than relying on my sometimes-faulty memory. Model railroad hook-up wire is of a heavy enough gauge to carry the required current while being of a small enough diameter to make it easy to thread through the tank's structure and light housings.

The speaker was relocated from the floor plate in the middle of the hull to aft in the engine compartment so the engine sounds would appear to be coming from the proper place. The servo for firing the "missile" from the gun was modified into a main gun elevation servo to move the gun up and down when it fires.

The kit's engine sound volume rheostat and knob did not have a scale appearance, so they were relocated from the outside top of the turret (where the spotlight mounts) to inside the battery compartment. Raising the engine access hatch and reaching inside allows access to the knob to adjust the volume when it's necessary. Nylon pressure-sensitive wire clips from the electronics store are peel-and-stick items which hold the various wiring harnesses in place in a neat and orderly manner. This kept my confusion to a minimum when I was attempting to sort out spaghetti-like wiring runs.

The various LEDs for the lighting circuits require resistors of certain values to step down the voltage to proper limits. A circuit board from the electronics store carries all the resistors required and is mounted on stand-offs made from sections of brass tubing. This allows cooling air to circulate beneath the board, since resistors get

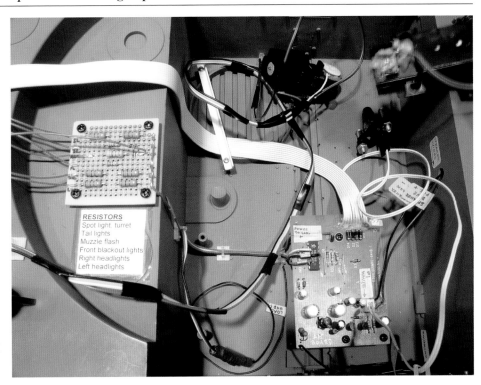

At the left: a circuit board from the electronics store has all the resistors for the LEDs in the lighting circuits installed on it. This is raised up on brass tubing stand-offs to allow for cooling air circulation since resistors get hot. A placard reminds me of what goes where.

hot. A label made on the computer reminds me of what the various resistors and wires are for when it comes time to connect it all up later. Important if you're me.

The main circuit off-on switch was relocated from its visible location on the aft upper hull to the inside of the driver's compartment to hide it. Reaching inside the driver's hatch allows access to the switch. I inform spectators whom I'm demonstrating the model to that–just as on the real tank–I'm turning on both ignition switches and hitting both engine starter buttons when I reach in the driver's

hatch for the switch. From their skeptical expressions I'm not certain they believe me. The sound board reproduces the sounds of the starter motors engaging, then both Cadillac™ engines firing up, and finally both engines settling down into a somewhat uneven idle. The engines roar to life when the radio transmitter asks for forward or aft movement of the vehicle. The volume control comes in handy if one wishes to do this late at night while playing with the model when other family members are trying to sleep. It doesn't do for a grown man to be caught playing.

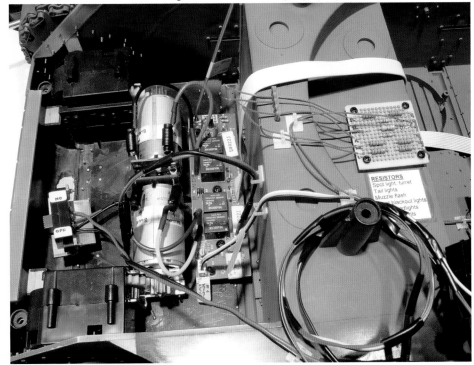

The various wiring runs are held in place by nylon wire clips which are pressure-sensitive and stick in place. This keeps the wiring harnesses neat and orderly so I can figure all this out later on in the project. At the left may be seen the drive motors, gear boxes, and forward PC board. The off-on switch has been relocated from the rear hull to the driver's compartment.

10

Modifying the Upper Hull in Stages

Stage 1 - Fenders

The sand shields had to be removed since *Cognac*–like most American M5A1 Stuarts–didn't have them. I used a Dremel tool with a separating disk slowed down by a rheostat to cut carefully along lines drawn on the shields. The cuts had rough edges since the disk partially melted the plastic (producing a very unpleasant smell), but a sanding block, files, and various grades of sanding sticks made things look better.

The front fenders that remained after the sand shields were cut off were far too thick and lacked scale fidelity and detail, so I decided to cut these away as well. To replace them I used .010 brass sheet for the fender pieces. The engineering drawings of the fenders were reduced to size on my computer and then were pasted on the brass sheet using rubber cement. An old pair of scissors easily cut the brass fenders out. Some minor curling of the brass occurred, but was taken care of by gently bending by hand and tapping both sides of the brass part with a nylon end of a craft

The sand shields and fenders were cut off the model using a Dremel Moto-tool with a separating disc. This is a messy operation which produces a rough cut requiring cleanup, plus an unpleasant smell, since the disk is partially melting the plastic.

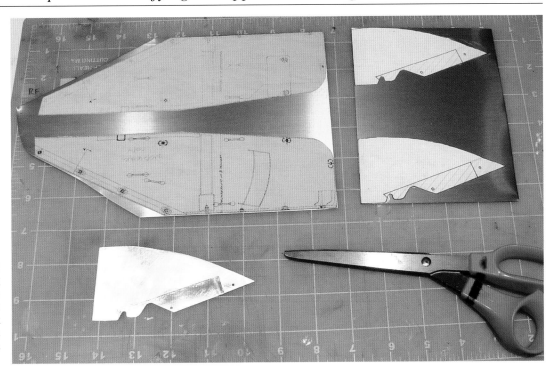

The new fenders were made from .010" sheet brass by first reducing the engineering drawings to size on a computer, then pasting the cut out forms on the brass sheet with rubber cement. Old scissors were used to cut out the brass pieces.

hammer over a jeweler's steel anvil. With a little patience the brass fender pieces straightened up nicely.

The brass fender pieces were soldered together using Stay-Brite™ silver solder and Stay-clean™ liquid flux. It proved helpful to have a Micro-Mark® ceramic fiber soldering pad to work on, since it was flame-proof and accepted straight pins easily which held some parts in place together during soldering. It's vital to keep parts to be soldered together absolutely stationary. A curved row of pins may be seen in the photo which held the fender side piece to the top piece during soldering. Also helpful was an X-ACTO X-TRA Hands™ clamping device that held the fenders while I soldered their rims around the pieces. I used K & S .015" x .060" brass strip for these rims, and this operation is shown.

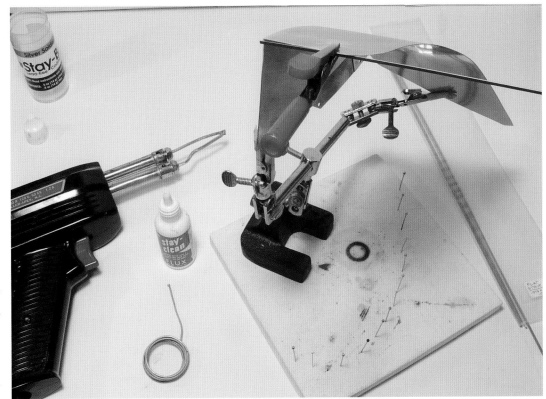

The brass fender pieces were held in an X-ACTO X-TRA Hands clamping device for soldering. Stay-Brite silver solder and Stay-Clean liquid flux were used for the soldering operations. The soldering was done over a Micro-Mark ceramic fiber soldering pad which easily accepts pins used to hold the brass parts in place, a vital necessity for soldering.

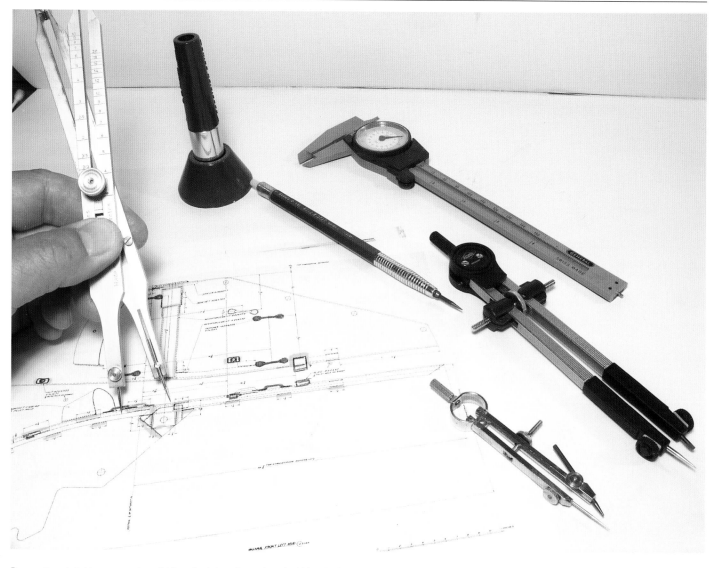

Proportional dividers proved useful for obtaining dimensions in 1/6 scale from plans drawn in another scale. Other useful tools for working with sheet brass are shown. The large and small compasses mark locations for drilling or bending a uniform distance from the edge.

Proportional dividers proved useful for obtaining dimensions in 1/6 scale from plans which were drawn in a different scale. These made it easy to construct parts that were dimensionally accurate from sheet brass. Other useful tools for working with sheet brass are a large and small compass. These come in handy to mark multiple locations a set distance from a certain reference point, for example, to mark locations on the sheet brass a uniform distance from the edge for drilling or bending. A draftsman's mechanical pencil with sharpener and a dial caliper were used frequently throughout this project. The dial caliper can measure the thickness of material from the outside, the clearance between parts from the inside, and the depth of a hole.

The scratch-built fenders made from .010" brass sheet were silver-soldered for strength. Reinforcing structure was added underneath from brass shapes, while the weld beads were made from 3M Acryl Green putty. The tie-down fittings are from Armorpax. The brush guard for the M2 tripod for the .30 caliber machine gun on the right fender was made up from .010" brass sheet bolted to nut plates made from sheet styrene and installed under the fenders. Hinge fittings for the sand shields were rolled from .015" brass sheet. The fenders were trial-fitted to the lower hull to verify fit prior to painting. They bolt up to the hull exactly as on the original tank using scale hardware. The unfinished upper hull is temporarily in place to check clearance. The right fender carries a brush guard for the .30 caliber tripod. The sheet brass fenders were primed and painted, and after receiving a coat of Testors Dullcote they were bolted to the lower hull.

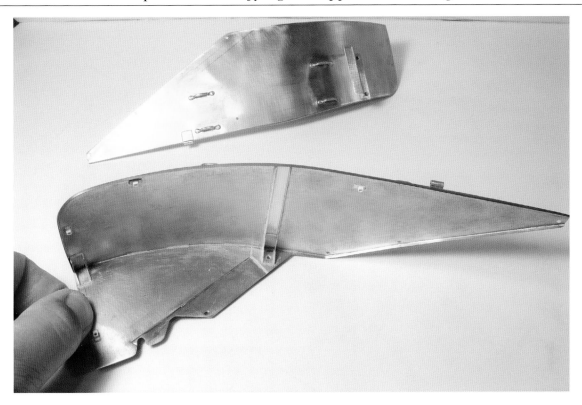

Scratch-built fenders made from .010" brass sheet were silver-soldered for strength. Structure was added underneath from brass shapes, weld beads made from 3M Acryl Green putty, and the tie-down fittings are from Armorpax.

The fenders were trial-fitted to the lower hull to verify fit prior to painting. They bolt up to the hull exactly as on the original using scale hardware. The unfinished upper hull is temporarily in place to check clearance. The right fender carries a brush guard for the .30 caliber tripod.

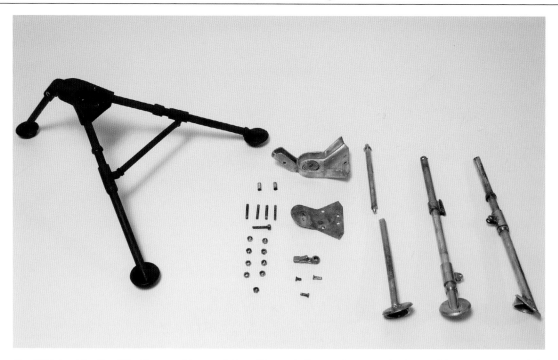

The M2 tripod for the .30 caliber machine gun is from Dragon in Dream. It was worked on at this stage to ensure it fit within the brush guard on the right front fender when folded. It was disassembled and stripped of paint.

The M2 tripod for the .30 caliber machine gun is from Dragon in Dream™. It was worked on at this stage to ensure that it fit within the brush guard on the right front fender when it was folded up. It was disassembled and stripped of its rough paint. The tripod was detailed with latches, springs, handles, foundry casting marks from Archer Fine Transfers™, and had the unauthentic seam under the tripod head silver-soldered to fill it. Weld beads were then made with 3M Acryl Green putty.

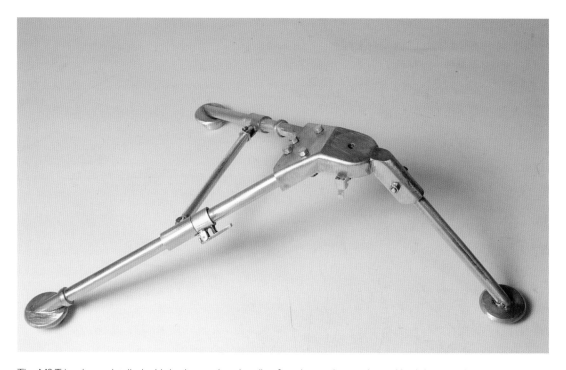

The M2 Tripod was detailed with latches, springs, handles, foundry casting marks, and had the unauthentic seam under the tripod head silver-soldered to fill it. Weld beads were then made with 3M Acryl Green putty.

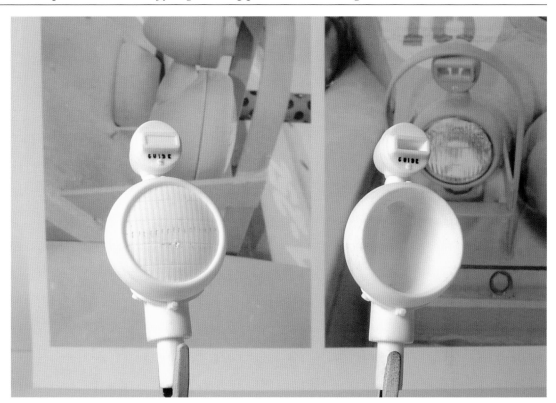

Resin headlight/blackout driving light assemblies from Panzerwerk were hollowed and drilled out to accept LEDs and wiring to make them operational.

Stage 2 - Headlights

Resin headlight/blackout driving light assemblies from Panzerwerk were hollowed out with a ball cutter used in a Dremel tool as the first step in making them operational. Holes had to be drilled in the bottom of the mounting pegs up through the headlights and into the blackout driving lights in order to insert the LEDs and their wiring. The original manufacturer's brand name (GUIDE) was made from raised resin letters taken from Archer Fine Transfers Sheet AR88007.

Reflectors from very small flashlights were cut down and modified to fit the headlights. A lens master was made from a .080" styrene disk which had the lens grid pattern cut and filed in. It was then vacuum-formed on an old Mattel® Vac-U-Form™ to make the two clear headlight lenses. To get a crisp vacuum-formed lens with sharp detail I found I had to drill a #79 hole at the intersection of every vertical and horizontal groove comprising the headlight lens' grid. This let air escape through these holes in the master, which then allowed the hot clear plastic to readily conform to the raised detail. The holes will not show on the final clear lens. A 5mm white LED and a 3mm yellow LED will be installed after the headlights are painted.

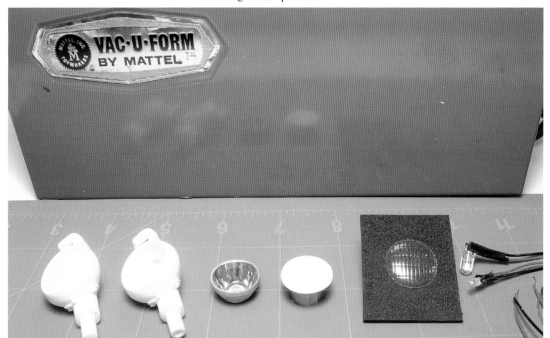

Reflectors from small flashlights were cut down and modified to fit the headlights. A lens master was made and then vacuum-formed for the two headlight lenses. Two LEDs at right await installation.

The LEDs and their wiring were operationally checked prior to painting the headlights.

The LEDs and their wiring were checked for operation prior to painting the headlights and to observe the quality of the vacuum-formed clear lens. The headlight/blackout driving lights were airbrushed, weathered, and received a protective coat of Testors Dullcote. The clear lenses were attached with diluted white glue. Any excess white glue can be easily cleaned up with a damp Q-tip (cotton bud). The lenses then received a seal coat of clear gloss. A lens for the blackout driving light was cut from a section of .020" clear acetate. Flat black was used to paint the inside of the lens to create the unique "cat's eye" driving light openings.

The painted and weathered headlight/blackout driving light unit with the clear lens attached.

The blackout driving light illuminated showing the "cat's eye" lens. To the left is the styrene master used to vacuum-form the clear lens.

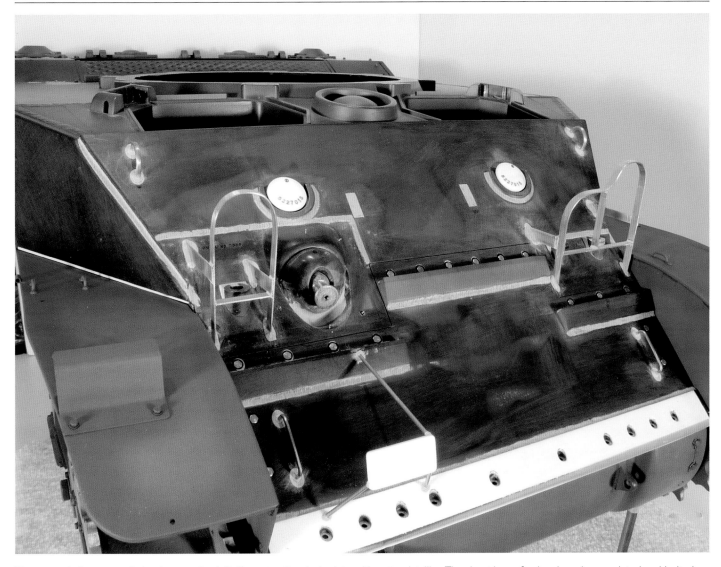

The upper hull temporarily in place to check fit illustrates the glacis plate with extra detailing. The sheet brass fenders have been painted and bolted on to the lower hull.

Stage 3 - Glacis plate

Extra detailing added to the upper hull's glacis plate included filling all unauthentic seams and sink holes with putty, creating numerous weld bead lines with Milliput that was textured with a dental spatula, and scribing in the recessed join line for the armored differential access plate using a scribing tool from Micro-Mark. This plate was detailed further by drilling out 17 shallow plastic bolt heads which held the real plate in place, then drilling holes for the installation of countersunk 1-72 brass hex head bolts. These were run into tapped holes. The plate's lower edge was built up with a .100" styrene strip installed transversely. This raised strip replaced the kit's one of inaccurate dimensions and it had ten holes bored in it. Brass 1-56 washers were placed in the countersunk holes used for the ten brass 1-56 bolts which will join the upper and lower hulls. The bolts screw into brass 1-56 hex nuts which will be visible under the lip of this access plate in front of the differential casting. Lifting handles for this plate were formed from .060" brass rod. A bullet deflector made from .100" sheet styrene and .060" brass rod was

fastened to the differential access plate in front of the bow machine gun. This item is of a controversial nature among the experts as to what it actually was. Most seem to agree it was a field modification unique to the 3rd Armored Division in Normandy. The idea was that the bow gunner could fire his .30 caliber machine gun into it, causing it to deflect a spray of unaimed rounds downward. This was important in keeping German heads down when the tank was exposing its vulnerable belly while in a nose-high attitude during the process of crashing through a hedgerow. The kit's brush guards for the headlights and siren were far too thick, lacked detail, and had to be replaced. The holes for their large screw-in mounts in the hull were filled with Milliput. New brush guards were formed from 3/16" x .030" strip brass for both headlights and the siren. Small weld beads on the pieces making up these assemblies were made using 3M Acryl Green body putty textured with a beveled toothpick. The bow machine gun mounting was filed, cut, and sculptured to a more accurate shape, and to give the machine gun a proper amount of elevation and deflection. The cut out section in the hull was filled in with Milliput, and an Armorpax ball mount was installed. The hull mount was drilled out for a set screw made from a 2-56 brass bolt which had its head cut off and a screwdriver slot cut in with a Dremel tool and a circular saw. The bow machine gun was replaced with a section of barrel cut from a 1/6 scale brass .30 caliber Browning M1919A4 machine gun from DiD. The armor mantlet over the barrel is from Armorpax. The spare bogie wheel was eliminated from the glacis plate and its mounting slots were filled in with Milliput. The shallow direct vision ports for the driver and assistant driver were cut away and replaced by thicker ones made of two disks of sheet styrene. These were detailed with foundry casting numbers and marks from Lion Roar and Archer. The hull lifting handles were made up from 1/16" brass rod with weld beads made from 3M Acryl Green body putty.

Stage 4 - Periscopes and hull hatches

The periscopes are resin castings from Panzerwerk which were highly modified. The circular groove on each periscope base that represented the separation of the inner and outer bearing races was repeatedly scored with a scriber from Micro-Mark until it separated. This allowed each periscope to swivel realistically within its bearing race once a pivot made from brass rod was installed.

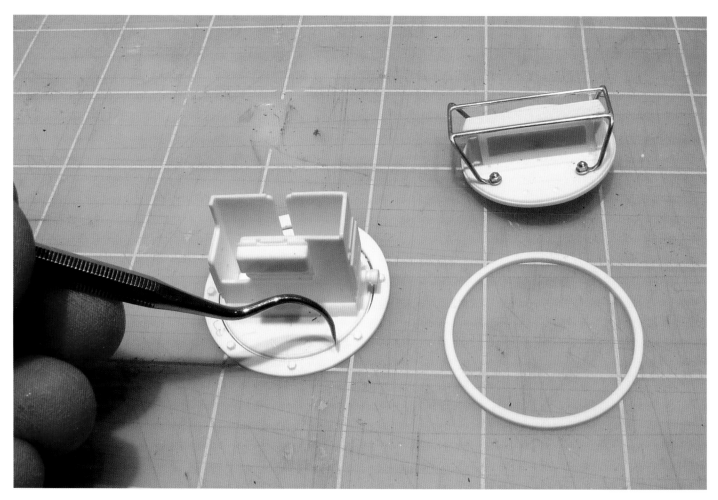

The Panzerwerk periscope bases were modified by using a scribing tool to repeatedly score the circular line representing the division between the inner and outer bearing races. Once separated, the periscopes were able to realistically swivel within their bearings.

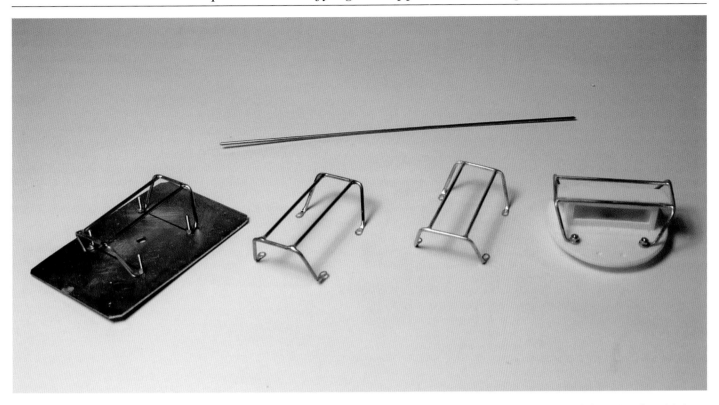

The stages of making periscope brush guards from .040" brass rod. A brass plate serves as a fixture to hold the pieces precisely in place for soldering.

Numerous holes were drilled into the interior mounts of the periscopes for added detail using photos for reference. The periscope prism housings were hollowed out with several sizes of ball cutters in a motor tool to allow installation of two mirrors in each. These mirrors were cut from strip styrene and were covered with Bare-Metal® aluminum foil. The upper mirror in each prism housing then had an added cover cut from exposed black and white film. This gave the periscope head a darker reflective interior which represents what you see when you look into an actual M6 periscope. Clear acetate was used to make the outer prism lenses. Brush guards were made for all the periscopes from .040" brass rod. The end sections were bent to shape over a wooden form, then the bolt pads were flattened out using a jeweler's brass hammer and a small modeler's anvil. Bolt holes were drilled, and then the pads were filed to shape using a sanding stick. A brass plate was made into a fixture for precisely locating the two cross pieces to the end pieces for soldering. The solder joints were cleaned up with sanding sticks, and then the guards were bolted to the periscopes using 00-90 bolts, washers, and nuts.

Many modifications were done to the driver's and bow gunner's hatches, including cutting out the solid hatch openings. The hull ventilator was cut out and a new ventilator dome was scratch-built.

The driver's and bow gunner's hatches were heavily modified for accuracy. The hatch openings were molded solid in the kit and had to be cut out. The hatch openings were detailed with sheet styrene fillets to make their outline shape more accurate. Strip styrene was used to make the padding around the inside of the hatch opening. The kit's bullet splash guards were not sharply molded and were cut away, then replaced with strip styrene ones. 3M Acryl Green body putty was used to make the small weld beads on the inside of the splash guards, while Milliput was used for the larger outside weld beads. The hatch hinges were reshaped by filing, adding sheet styrene pieces, and having their unauthentic openings and holes filled with Milliput. The hatch hinge mounts on the hull were heavily reshaped with sheet styrene pieces and by

filing. The hatch hinge pins were made from brass rod and have coil springs made from wound wire. The inside faces of the hatches were detailed with bullet splash guards made from strip styrene with putty weld beads. Closing handles and latch pins made from brass rod were also added. Foundry casting numbers were added to these components using the Lion Roar brass photoetch sheets. The hull ventilator between the driver and bow gunner hatches was cut out, the resulting hole filled with a sheet styrene plug, and a new ventilator dome was laminated up from sheet styrene. Foundry casting numbers and marks were added from Lion Roar and Archer, and two drain holes were drilled in the front of its circular bullet splash guard. Weld beads were made from putty and Milliput.

A close-up of the driver's hatch with highly-modified Panzerwerk periscopes, bullet splash guards, hatch opening fillets to correct the shape, and other details.

Scanning an actual M6 periscope to obtain an image of its data plate in order to make small decals for the model periscopes.

An actual full-size M6 periscope was scanned in order to obtain an image of its data plate. This image was enhanced on the computer using Microsoft® Office Picture Manager™, and then reduced to approximately 9% of its original size. This small image was copied a dozen times, then printed on white decal paper. After over coating these images with Testors Dullcote, each was cut out and applied to each periscope as a water slide decal.

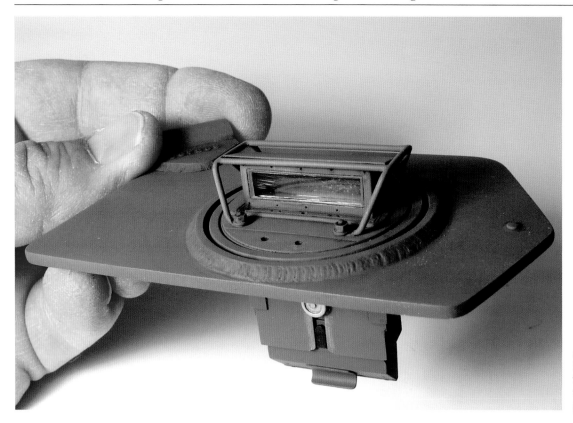

A view of the outside of the bow gunner's hatch showing the finished periscope. Acetate was used to make the outside glass.

The hatches for the driver and bow gunner were painted, along with the periscopes to be mounted on them, and were then assembled and placed away for assembly at a later time.

An inside view of the finished driver's hatch showing the periscope in its mount.

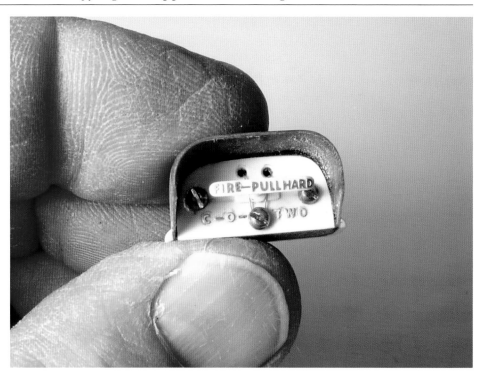

The fire extinguisher T-handle and its mount were scratch-built and will sit outside the hull on the right, aft of the turret. The lettering is the smallest size on the Lion Roar sheets.

Stage 5 - Hull midsection

The hull-mounted fire extinguisher housing was carved and hollowed out to an accurate shape from its solid rectangular form. The T-handle was shaped from strip styrene, a rear wall was made of sheet styrene, small brass screw heads were added, and the lettering is the smallest size from the Lion Roar sheets of photoetch letters.

The hull turret ring was detailed with foundry casting numbers and marks on each segment between the bearing housings, and each segment had a weld bead made of Milliput added. Each bearing housing had the two round molded-on bolt heads drilled out, plastic plugs added at the bottom of the resulting holes, and brass 2-56 bolts, nuts, and washers were added into drilled and tapped holes. This improved their scale appearance greatly. A round blanking plate for an unused radio antenna mount located on the hull's upper surface on the right was made from sheet styrene. This was detailed with foundry casting numbers and marks. It has a circular bullet splash guard made from .060" x .060" square brass bar bent to shape. Brass oval head wood screws which attached the side hull armor plates replaced the kit's molded-on bumps representing screws. The upper sand shield hinges on the hull sides were made from brass strip bent to shape around brass rod.

Parts, hardware, and modifications to the turret ring and engine deck are visible here. The hinged engine access cover was made more accurate by cutting the two forward panels from the hull (all three should be one integral unit) and joining them to the cover.

The engine access cover hinges up and aft to reveal the battery compartment. A sheet styrene box structure fills the voids where the two forward panels were cut from the hull. This restores the hull's rigidity.

Stage 6 - Forward engine deck

The kit depicted the engine compartment top door, or cover, incorrectly by molding it far too short in the fore-and-aft direction. Using an X-ACTO micro saw blade I cut out the missing two panels of the door from the hull top and attached them to the engine cover so that all three would open together as one integral door. The X-ACTO micro saw blade fits either way into a #1 hobby knife handle (the smaller of the two handles X-ACTO makes), with your choice of saw teeth facing forward or backwards. To insert the saw blade into the thick plastic of the hull to begin a cut I drill a number of holes with a #70 drill in a line along the intended cut a bit more than the height of the blade. I then drill the plastic out between the holes I've made. This opens up a thin slot into which you can insert the saw blade and begin sawing away. After removing the sawn-out panels from the hull, the resulting voids in the hull were boxed in with .060" sheet styrene to restore the hull's rigidity. A side benefit of this was the boxed-in area accurately depicts the space where the two radiators would lie. These were represented by sheet styrene pieces covered with brass screening. Much of the kit's oversize or overly simple details on the engine deck, such as grab handles, were replaced with ones made from brass rod, and the many bump-like bolts on the hull were replaced with brass 2-56 bolts. Resin engine compartment cover hinges from Panzerwerk replaced the oversize hinges of the kit which were cut off, and the new hinges have hinge pins made from brass rod with details cut into their ends. The solid cooling air intake screen, which was molded on in the kit, was cut away with the micro saw. The intake area was boxed in with sheet styrene and has a transverse slot for the cooling air to travel down through the radiators located below. The engine access hatch will now open to allow access to the battery compartment, which holds the 12 volt 7 AH (amp hour) battery that powers the tank's electrical system. The engine sound volume control mentioned previously was installed in this compartment to hide it.

The frame for the forward engine air intake was silver-soldered up from K & S brass L-angle shapes over a balsa wood form cut to size. The balsa proved too weak for the forces involved and I used basswood for this hereafter. Pins hold the assembly firmly in place during soldering.

The frame for the forward engine air intake was silver-soldered up from K & S 1/16" brass L-angle shapes over a balsawood form cut to size to fit the intake opening. Experience would soon teach me that balsa was not dense and sturdy enough for the forces involved, so I would later use basswood for the aft intake screen form. Pins hold the assembly firmly in place during soldering, a key element in precision soldering.

AMACO Copper WireForm® mesh in the smaller size of 1/16" is cut to shape and held in place with a single-edge razor blade while gluing down with cyanoacrylate glue, which is applied with a wire applicator.

AMACO copper WireForm mesh in the smaller 1/16" size is cut to shape and held in place with a single-edge razor blade while gluing down with cyanoacrylate glue which was applied with a wire applicator.

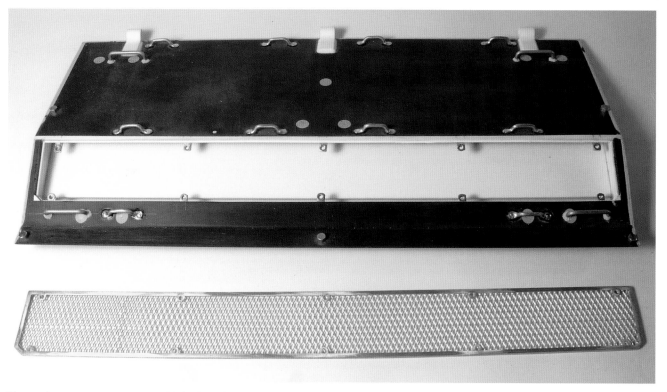

The engine compartment cover with its boxed-in air intake plenum has threaded attachment pads made from .030" × 1/16 brass strip. The completed intake screen frame will bolt directly to these.

The engine compartment cover, with its boxed-in air intake plenum, had threaded attachment pads made from .030" x 1/16 brass strip. The completed intake screen frame will screw in directly to these using scale 2-56 hex head bolts. Once in place, the engine compartment cover screen still reveals the extent of the boxed-in plenum beneath it, along with the transverse slot, which allows a view of the two radiators underneath.

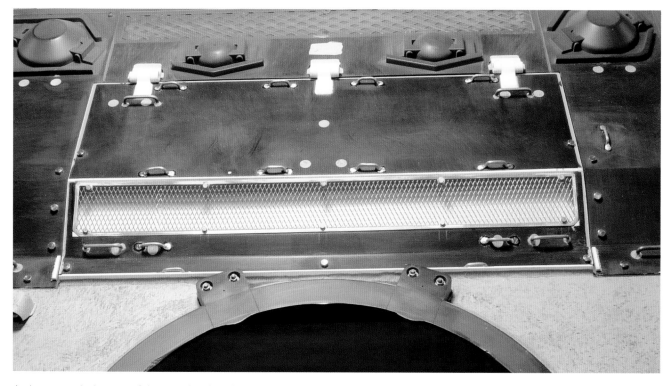

A view towards the rear of the completed engine compartment cover with the intake screen in place showing the boxed-in plenum with a transverse slot revealing the two radiators beneath.

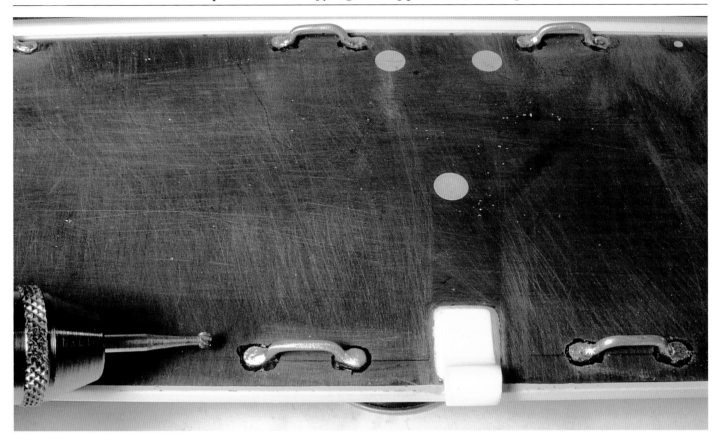

The cast metal tie-down fittings (or footman's loops) from Armorpax have large raised rounded ends with fastener heads which were not used on the Stuart. These were ground down with a ball cutter in a rough manner to replicate the spot welds attaching the tie-downs to the engine compartment cover.

The cast metal tie-down fittings from Armorpax are very nice castings, but these have raised rounded ends that are too large. They also include fastener heads that were used on some vehicles, but not on the Stuart, which were welded in place without fasteners. To replicate the flat spot welds used to attach these to the vehicle the ends were ground down with a ball cutter in a powered hobby tool in a rough manner, a quick and easy process once the tie-downs were installed.

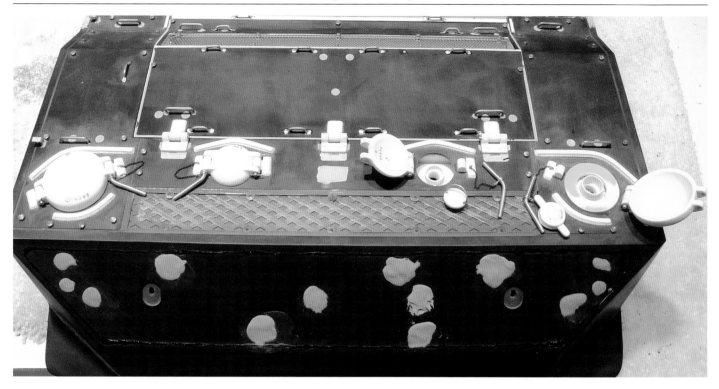

The kit's toy-like armored covers for the fuel and radiator caps were cut off and replaced with resin items from Panzerwerk. The six bullet splash guards were part of this replacement kit. The armor cover hinge pins and locking handles were made from brass rod and were secured with chains.

Stage 7 - Radiator caps and fuel tank caps

The molded-on armored covers for the two radiator caps were too small in diameter, and the hinges for these and for the two fuel caps were overly simplified and looked toy-like. Fortunately a replacement kit for these is available from Panzerwerk which also includes six bullet splash guards, all cast in resin. A nice feature of this detailed kit is the inclusion of the radiator caps and fuel caps which sit on filler neck units that are installed under the armor caps. After the kit's parts were cut and sanded off, the Panzerwerk instructions were followed for the installation of the new resin items. Resin hinge pins and locking handles were provided, but these were cast slightly out of round, so I decided to make better ones from .060" brass rod. The hinge pins were secured in place

with cotter pins made from .015" brass strip, while the locking handles are secured by lengths of chain attached to eyebolts made from brass wire. The radiator caps had resin handles which were cut off in order to have replacement handles made of brass wire which attach to and swivel on brass tabs cemented to the caps. These were much stronger than the cast resin handles and can now be used to twist off the radiator caps and lock them back on their filler necks. A slight modification to these caps allows their lower tabs to engage slots in the filler neck so they can be rotated to lock in place. The fuel caps were thinned inside to allow them to twist down on their filler necks and lock in place by friction. Foundry casting numbers for the armor covers, fuel caps, and radiator caps were obtained from the Lion Roar photoetch sheets.

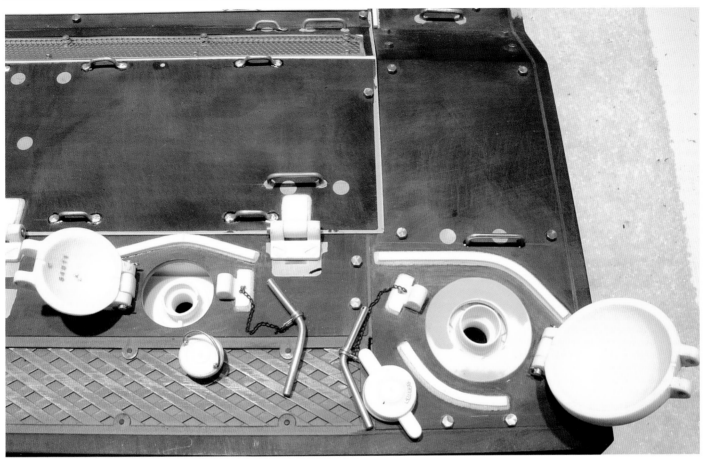

The armored covers open up after withdrawing the locking handles, and the radiator and fuel caps unscrew, revealing the filler necks underneath. Cotter pins made from brass strip secure the hinge pins. Photoetch foundry casting numbers were added to the covers and caps.

All of this surgery on the fuel and radiator caps is hindered by the adjacent bullet splash guards, so these are best cut off the engine deck to create more working room. Fortunately, replacements for the splash guards are included in the Panzerwerk kit, and these have a much better scale appearance.

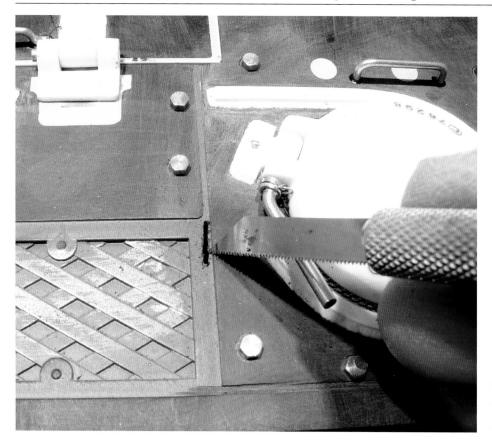

To cut out the unauthentic aft engine air intake a series of .015" holes were drilled in a line to create a slot into which an X-ACTO micro saw could be inserted to complete the cuts.

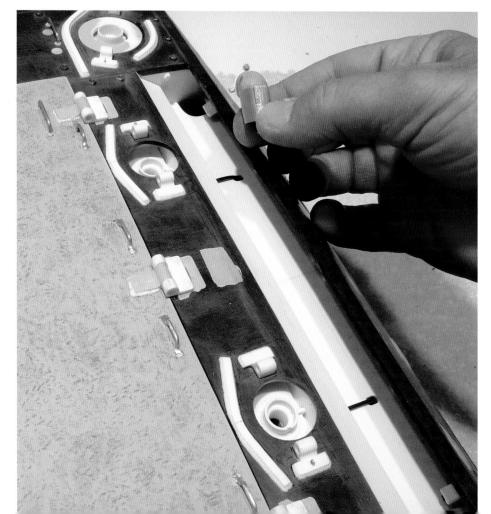

The aft engine air intake plenum was boxed in with sheet styrene and has details added such as nuts, bolts, radiator overflow hoses, and carburetor intake pipes.

Stage 8 - Aft engine deck

The aft engine cooling air intake was cut out the same way as the forward one. First, a series of .015" holes are drilled in a line to create a slot into which an X-ACTO micro saw can be inserted. Then the saw cut is made. It's best to cut inside the final lines first, and then use sanding sticks and files to widen the opening out to the final lines.

After cleaning up the edges of the opening, the area was boxed in with .060" sheet styrene to create the plenum for the aft cooling air intake. Items within will be quite visible, so reference photos were used to create details, such as nuts, bolts, radiator overflow hoses made from black electrical wire, and carburetor intake elbows. Brass tubing and Milliput epoxy putty were used to create the basic shape for the elbows, and then smaller details were added, such as bolts, bolt flange, and foundry casting numbers.

The completed aft engine air intake screen and frame was bolted down in place over the boxed-in plenum to check fit and placement and the need for any adjustment. This assembly is far more realistic than the kit's original "basket-weave" screen, which was cut out and discarded.

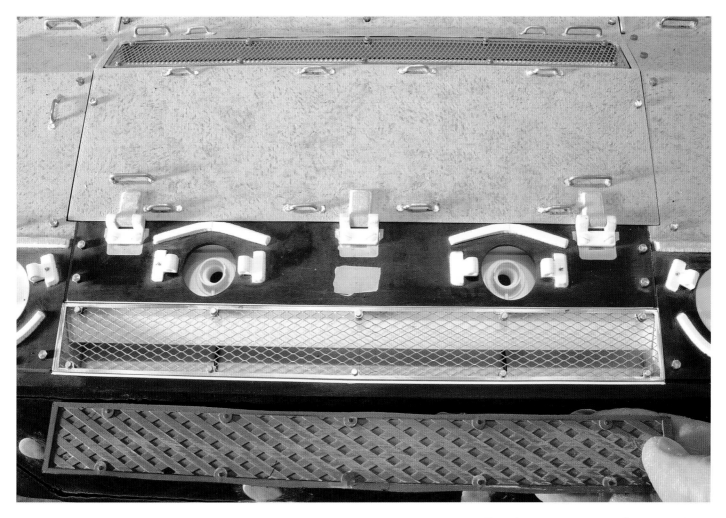

The completed aft engine air intake screen and frame bolted down in place over the boxed-in plenum. The kit's original "basket-weave" screen which was cut out and replaced is shown below the new screen.

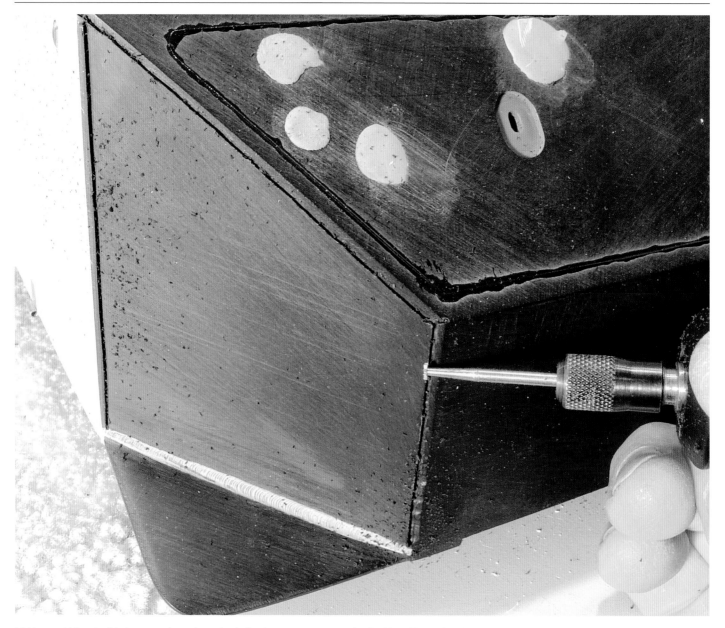

Making weld beads #1-A groove is cut into the hull using a rotary cutter chucked in a Dremel tool. This provides an anchor for the Milliput epoxy putty making up the weld bead.

Stage 9 - Aft hull quarter panels
Making weld beads

1. All weld beads on the kit were replaced with more authentic appearing ones, and in many places beads had to be created where the kit depicted none. This included the hull aft quarter panels. The methods for making these weld beads are easy to do. To make a weld bead from Milliput epoxy putty it's best to provide a groove for the putty to adhere to. This is done with a small rotary cutter chucked in a powered hobby tool, in this case a Dremel Moto-tool. Running the cutter at a relatively slow speed using Dremel's Speed Control (a type of rheostat) avoids melting the plastic of the hull.

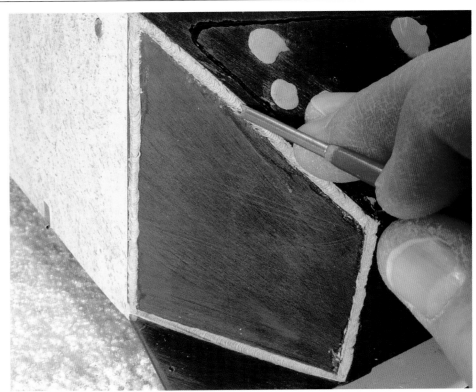

Making weld beads #2-The Milliput is rolled into a thin strip and placed over the groove. It's tamped into place using a homemade tool made up from brass tubing sliced at an angle and glued to an old paint brush handle. This creates the bead's semi-circular lapped texture.

2. The Milliput is rolled into small diameter strips and applied to the groove on the hull, then tamped in place with wet fingers. A homemade beading tool is used to create the semicircular lapped weld beads. This was made from a section of brass tubing with ½" of the upper surface ground away at the working end, and then the end was cut off at a 45 degree angle. The tubing was then glued into a used paint brush handle. Keeping the beading end of the tool wet keeps the Milliput from sticking to it.

3. Weld beads which lie within an inside angle are best textured using a dental spatula, again keeping it wet.

Making weld beads #3-Beads which lay in an inside angle are textured with a dental spatula kept slightly wet to avoid the putty sticking to it. This tool makes lovely semi-circular lapped texture weld beads.

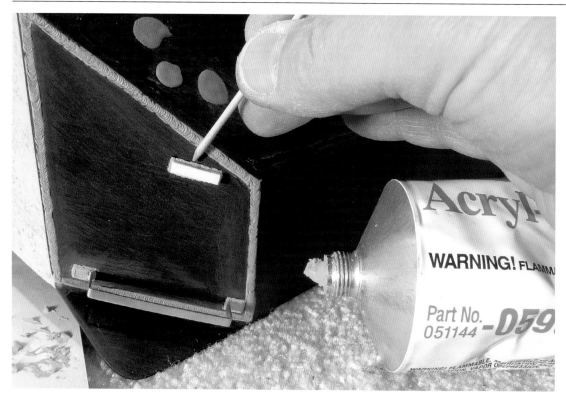

Making weld beads #4-Smaller beads are more easily made with 3M Acryl Green body putty applied with a wet toothpick and then textured.

4. Smaller weld beads are more easily made using body putty, since it can be difficult to roll the Milliput into very small diameter beads. A wet toothpick is used to apply and texture 3M Acryl Green body putty for small weld beads.

A Hold and Fold tool™ from The Small Shop™ is useful for bending up parts made from brass sheet and strip, including the spare track block clamps. The part is clamped in the appropriate place on the bending tool, and then a single-edge razor blade is used to bend the part up to the proper angle. Using the razor blade ensures sharp small-radius bends.

A "Hold and Fold" tool from The Small Shop is useful for bending up parts made from brass sheet and strip.

A view of the hull's left rear panel showing several types of weld beads. The spare track blocks are held in place by a bracket and clamp made up from brass strip and sheet which was then bolted in place.

The squared-off rear fenders were reshaped in plan view at this time to conform to plans and photos, necessary once the sand skirts were removed. They also had their edges thinned so as to appear as thinner sheet metal. The completed aft hull quarter panel includes details, such as different types of weld beads, spare track blocks in their brackets and bolted-on clamps, and fenders which have two holes drilled in for attaching the sand skirts that were removed.

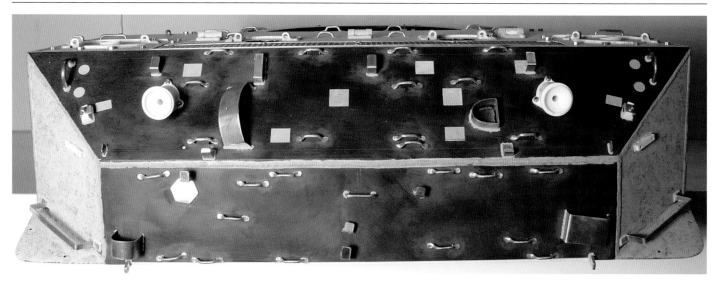

The aft hull plates with details: white metal tie-downs from Armorpax, resin taillights from Panzerwerk, and scratch-built brass hull lifting loops, fittings, and racks for the various tools. Milliput putty fills the holes left by removal of the many unauthentic kit tie-downs and tool clamps.

Stage 10 - Aft hull plates

The two aft hull plates had all their unauthentic details removed and the resulting holes were filled with Milliput. New details were added, such as white metal tie-downs from Armorpax and scratch-built hull lifting rings, fittings, and racks for the various tools made from brass rod, strip, and sheet. Resin taillights from Panzerwerk replaced the simplified ones in the kit, and these were modified by cutting off their molded-on bolt heads and replacing them with brass 00-90 bolts and washers. Foundry casting numbers were added to the side of the taillight housings, and the name of the original manufacturer (GUIDE) was added to the light end caps below the lenses. The solid lenses were opened up and replaced with clear and translucent red lenses made from acetate. The kit's

simplified weld beads were sanded off and replaced with new ones made from Milliput.

White metal tools from Armorpax were added, including a mattock head, mattock handle, shovel, sledge hammer, and axe. A pry bar came with this set, but it was too short according to plans and photos, so the white metal handle was cut off and replaced with a section of brass rod of the proper length. The Armorpax tool set also included a track tensioning tool (wrench), and this fits the three nuts on each of the idler wheel arms that are used to adjust the track tension by moving the idler wheel fore or aft. This wrench is used on the model for this, just as on the actual tank. The tools are removable, and will be held in place later by leather straps with buckles. On either side of the upper aft hull plate are clamped two scratch-built track fixtures made from sheet styrene.

The aft hull with the tools added: top left is a mattock head; top middle is the mattock handle; below that is a shovel, below that is a pry bar with a brass rod handle, below that is an axe, track tensioning wrench, and a sledge hammer. The tools are removable. On the left and right are scratch-built track fixtures in white styrene.

The track fixtures were scratch-built from styrene and have brass bolts and photoetch foundry casting numbers and manufacturer's data. The fixture hooks are adjustable for track width. Below are the kit's track fixtures which were replaced.

Two track fixtures were scratch-built from styrene and replaced the kit's overly simplified ones. The sliding hooks are secured with 0-80 brass bolts that had their hexagonal heads filed to a square head shape. The brass photoetch foundry casting numbers and manufacturer's data came from the Lion Roar photoetch sheets. The fixture hooks are adjustable for track width.

These track fixtures are used on the real tank to draw together the ends of a split track in order to join them. Two are required to splice a track, and they are drawn together by a ratcheting screw jack which hooks into square openings in the fixtures. This jack is represented in the photo by a toothpick.

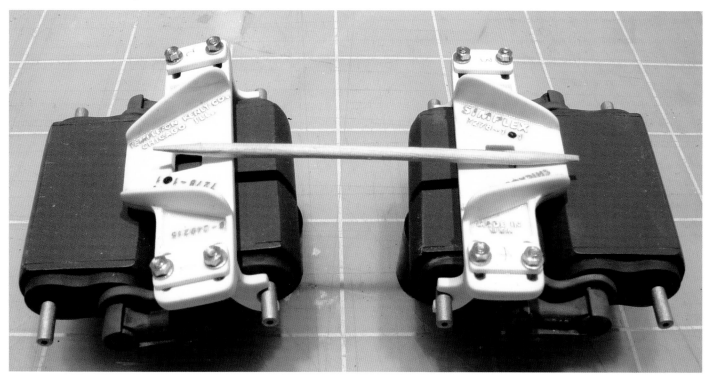

How the track fixtures work: two are required to join a split track and are drawn together by a ratcheting screw jack which hooks into the square openings in the fixtures, represented here by a wooden stick.

11

Painting the Upper Hull

A large debris field was created by all the cut-off and discarded parts from the kit at this stage of construction. It was fun to watch the pile grow, but I realized each piece represented another item which had to be scratch-built, a visible reminder of just how much time I had put into this project. The turret discards (not shown here) would add greatly to this large landfill.

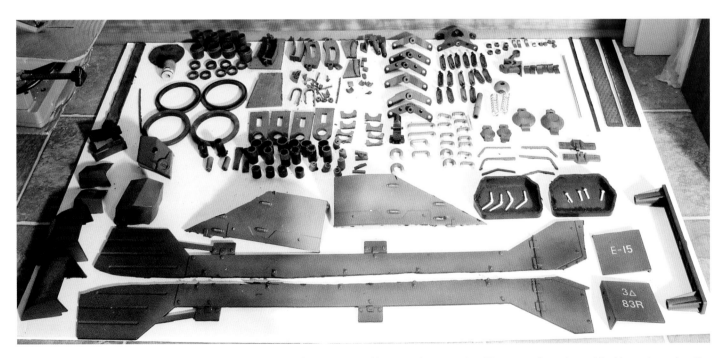

The debris field created by all the cut-off and discarded parts from the kit at this stage of construction. The turret discards would add greatly to the pile.

The model was becoming too heavy to hold while working on it and it was necessary to construct a work stand which could rotate. This was made from a TV tray table and a shelf I cut in two which sandwiched a 10" lazy susan bearing from a home improvement store.

The model was becoming too heavy to hold while working on it, and it became necessary to construct a work stand which could rotate. This would make it much easier to detail and paint various sections of the model. This stand was made from an inexpensive–yet very sturdy–TV tray which I obtained (along with everything else needed to make it) from my local do-it-yourself store. I added castering wheels to the legs of the tray to enable it to move easily across the floor. A 36" length of Melamine shelving was cut into two halves to become the upper and lower sections of a rotating Lazy Susan, and I dressed up the sawn edges with white trim iron-on veneer. For rotation I screwed a 10" Lazy Susan bearing to the

upper and lower pieces of shelving. Now the model was positioned at a comfortable height for working on and had the capability to rotate 360 degrees to enable me to work easily on any part of it. Not having to hold the model constantly made the project not only more fun but much less fatiguing. Another benefit of not having to constantly hold such a large model is that you reduce the risk of breaking parts off while you wrestle with it. It's vital, of course, to choose a sturdy enough tray that won't collapse under the ever-growing weight of the model. To wit: this model of a "light" tank would eventually weigh in at a not inconsiderable 32 lbs. (14.5 kg.).

The unit assignment markings are dry transfers from Woodland Scenics. The armor triangles were made from using three transfers of the letter "I" which were trimmed to shape. The marking reads "3rd Armored Division, 33rd Armored Regiment, Company C, tank 32".

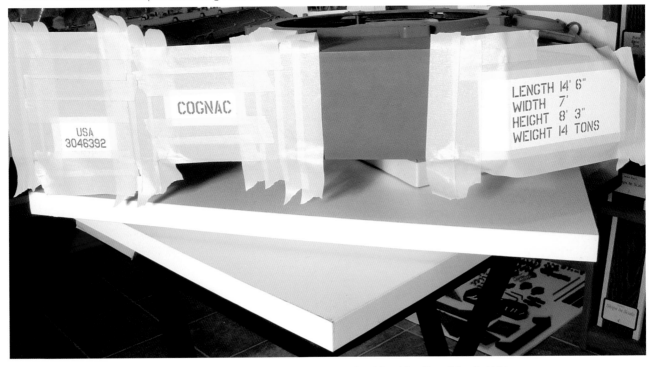

Vinyl stencils in place and masked further, ready for airbrushing Floquil Reefer White.

The tactical marking "C-32" was first sized up on the computer to 204 points from a military stencil font, then printed out. Grafix frisket film was laid over this image, taped down, and a stencil was cut out with a hobby knife with a new #11 blade using a straight edge.

The upper hull was painted in accordance with the painting schedule described in Chapter 7 and left to dry for several days to allow the paint to fully harden and cure. The unit assignment markings are dry transfers from Woodland Scenics. The armor symbols (triangles) were made from three capital "I" letters, then trimmed and touched-up with paint. The marking reads "3rd Armored Division, 33rd Armored Regiment, Company C, tank 32".

Stencils from GetStencils.com™ were taped in place for painting, and Floquil Reefer White was airbrushed on.

The tactical marking "C-32" (Company C, tank 32) was first sized up on the computer to 204 points from a military stencil font then printed out. Grafix® frisket film was laid over this image,

taped down, and a stencil was cut out with a hobby knife with a new #11 blade using a straight edge. The backing was peeled away from the frisket film, exposing its adhesive, and the stencil was then applied to the model. It's a good idea to burnish down the edges of the stencil's lettering to ensure paint doesn't bleed under the film. It's also better to spray several light semi-dry coats of paint rather than one wet coat to eliminate any possibility of paint bleeding under the stencil. This tactical marking was sprayed with Floquil Reefer Yellow that was lightened with some white to make it less vivid for enhanced scale effect. The markings came out almost perfectly and required only very minor touch-up when dry. They were then sealed with a coat of Testors Dullcote which was airbrushed over the entire upper hull. Using vinyl stencils is explained in detail in Chapter 12.

A view of the finished airbrushed markings. The "C-32" was sprayed with Floquil Reefer Yellow lightened with some white to make it less vivid for scale effect. The markings required only minor touch-up when dry, then were airbrushed with Testors Dullcote.

The upper hull was temporarily put in place over the lower hull to check fit, finish, and to complete the wiring from all the lights. Enough slack was left in the wiring harness to allow the upper hull to be removed and laid aside with the harness intact. It's starting to look like a tank!

The upper hull was temporarily put in place over the lower hull to check fit, finish, and to complete the wiring connections from all the lights. Enough slack was left in the wiring harness to allow the upper hull to be removed and laid aside with the harness intact. This will be necessary when the time comes to attach the completed turret. Hey! It's beginning to look like a tank!

The 15-ton bridge classification marking was made by cutting a stencil from frisket film with a circle cutter, then airbrushing it yellow. The numbers came from a dry transfer set. The mirror allows viewing of details under the hull without the necessity of picking up the model, which is very heavy in any case.

The 15-ton bridge classification marking was made by cutting a stencil from frisket film with a compass-type circle cutter, applying it to the glacis plate, and then airbrushing it yellow. The numbers came from a dry transfer set. An inexpensive custom mirror was cut at the hardware store and lies on the base under the model. The mirror's sharp edges were trimmed for safety with flying model airplane tape in yellow to match the tank's tactical marking. The mirror makes all the detail under the hull much more visible, disinclining interested modelers from attempting to pick up this heavyweight.

12

Turret Work Begins

I spent quite a bit of time working on the turret interior, most of it unplanned as sort of an afterthought. Initially I was not going to put an interior in the turret, since some of the radio control mechanism and wiring was there taking up room and was very visible through the open hatches. Then I made the fatal mistake of deciding I could at least scratch-build the SCR-508 radio to fill out the inside of the turret bustle. When that was done I thought I could add one more thing, then one more, and then quite before I knew it I had lost control. Having come this far, I felt I might as well finish the job and do the full interior as best I could. This process took several months and set the project back by that amount of time, but in the end I was pleased to have done it. The two turret hatches are large and permit viewing of the whole turret interior. The size of

this model is such that it would seem incomplete without having a full interior, so I bowed to the inevitable and sallied forth to do battle with all the complexities involved in this undertaking. The process of creating a scale interior around the radio control gear and cutting away most of the unauthentic strengthening webs inside the turret to create the room to do this was challenging, but when I viewed the finished interior through the hatches I wondered why I could possibly have entertained *not* doing this.

The turret mounting ring required a strip of styrene glued around its periphery to act as a shim to enlarge its diameter to eliminate the turret wobbling within the hull opening. The turret skirt underneath the bustle had no flare outwards and downwards like the rest of the skirt, but rather appeared as a vertical wall. This

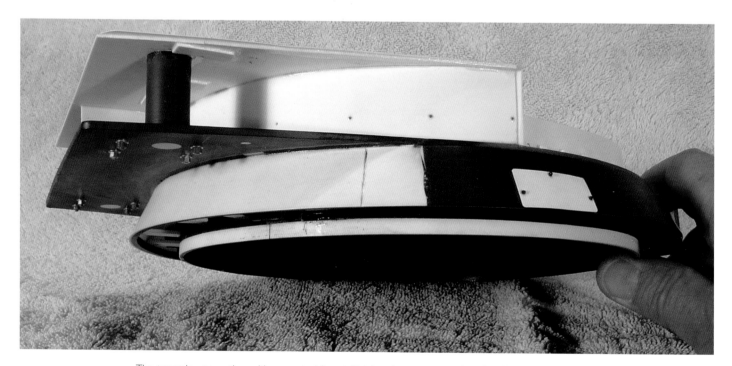

The turret lower section with corrected flared skirt, bearing access panel, and radio shelf in the bustle.

vertical section was cut away, and the proper flare was created with .040" sheet styrene. The skirt was shaped and braced in this position by eight .040" sheet styrene formers glued around the periphery of the turret's aft side inboard of the skirt. Forward of this new flared section on the right side of the turret skirt I added an access panel with three screws, which on the full size tank was removable to allow changing out the turret support bearings. Underneath the bustle I filled several unauthentic holes with styrene plugs, and then added eight 1-72 brass bolts, washers, and nuts representing the hardware used to bolt down the radio equipment located above and inside the turret.

Turret interior

A turret basket was made from .040" sheet styrene, which provided a base for all the floor-mounted components and equipment. Due to the design of the turret mounting, the ring of teeth comprising the traverse rack, and the electrical traverse motor I was unable to mount the turret basket a scale depth down into the hull. Using perspective to alter the size and relationship of certain interior items, I was able to construct a convincing facsimile of the turret interior while preserving the radio control operations of the kit. This was a compromise I was not fully comfortable with, but it was one that allowed the turret interior to be completed. I found that most viewers don't notice this because of the large amount of detail and equipment in the turret which attracts their attention first, so I suppose I can learn to live with it.

Different thicknesses of sheet styrene and brass sheet, along with differing diameters of brass rod and styrene rod were used to make up the seat mounts and tracks, ammunition cases and shell holders, turret master switch, spotlight stowage mount, the SCR-508 radio shelf, and other details. Many bolt heads were made by slicing off sections of Plastruct hexagonal rod in .060", .080", and .100" diameters. The SCR-508 radio was scratch-built from sheet styrene and rod in various sizes. This radio is comprised of three units: a BC-604 FM transmitter and two BG-603 FM receivers. Also made were an FT-237 mount and an A-62 phantom antenna from brass tubing. This phantom antenna allowed tuning of the radio without sending out a traceable signal.

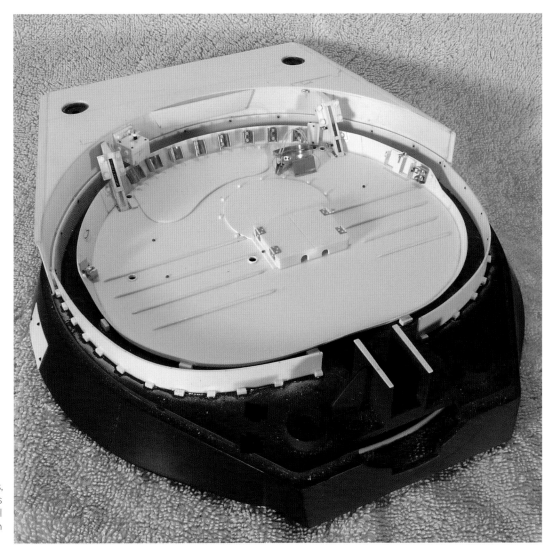

The turret basket and components, including the brass 37mm shell clips in a row towards the rear. Liberal use is made of sheet styrene in this phase of construction.

A view of several items for the turret interior, including the SCR-508 radio, spotlight cord reel, turret control panel, and intercom box.

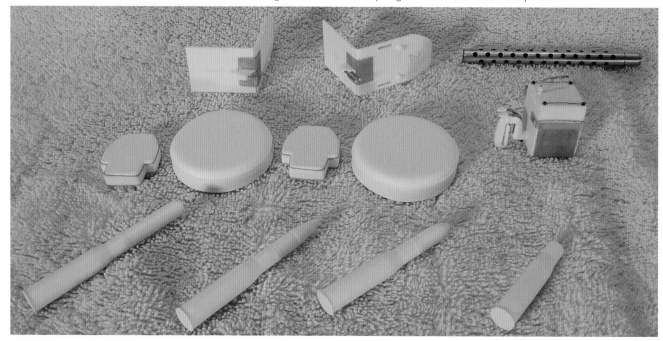

Sheet styrene used singly and laminated up into thicker sections made up the seat frames, seat and back cushions, and turret traverse control box. The Panzerwerk 37mm rounds are in the foreground.

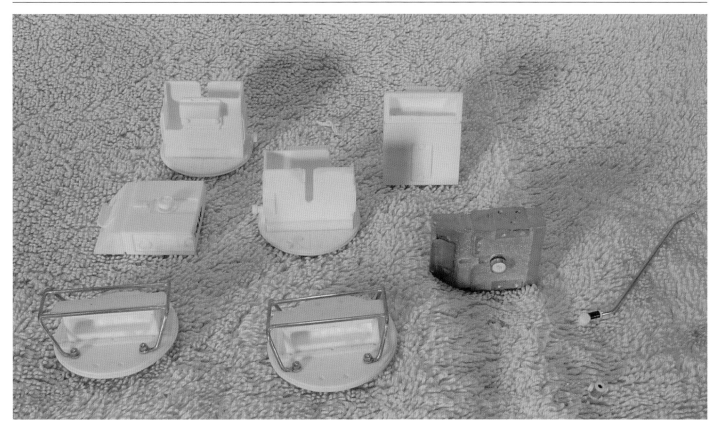

The Panzerwerk periscopes and guards made from brass rod will be installed in the turret.

A cord reel for the spotlight was made up from laminated sheet styrene with photoetch foundry casting numbers and the manufacturer's name "CORDOMATIC" made up from the Lion Roar photoetch sheets. Box structures were made up from sheet styrene, including the turret electrical control panel and an intercom switch panel.

The seat frames were made from sheet styrene, while the seat and back cushions were formed from laminated sheet styrene. The cushions have seams and beaded edges made from .010" styrene rod. A brass .30 caliber machine gun barrel from Dragon in Dream was stripped and polished and replaced the plastic coaxial gun in the kit. The turret traverse control box and handle with triggers were made up from sheet styrene, brass sheet, and have safety-wired screws. Four resin 37mm rounds came from Panzerwerk.

Illustrated are an M2 canister round (which contained 122 steel balls, a lethal and not-very-nice anti-personnel weapon), an M51 armor piercing capped round, an M74 armor piercing round, and an empty shell, which will be placed in the 37mm gun's shell collection bag. All four shell cases had new rims made from .010" sheet styrene to replace the chipped resin ones. The primer pockets were scribed in the shell bases.

Two resin periscopes from Panzerwerk were added to the turret, made up identically to the two previously described which were installed in the hull hatches. One cast metal periscope from Armorpax was detailed and will be stowed in its box mounted inside the turret on the right wall. Brass rod and various bits of round and hexagonal styrene rod were used to make up the link connecting the gunner's sighting periscope with the 37mm gun.

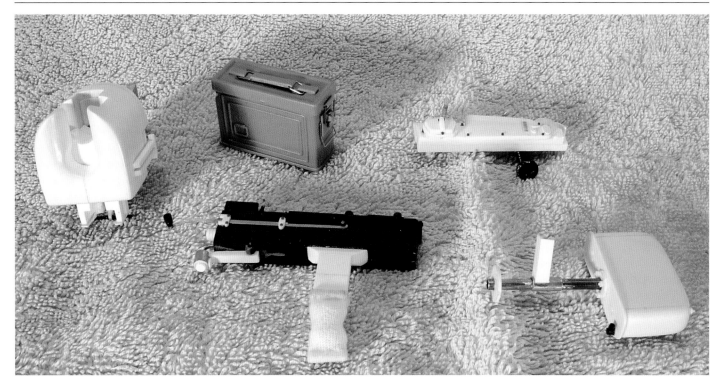

Various components for the 37mm gun: the breech ring with sliding breech, .30 caliber ammunition can, manual turret traverse mechanism, and gyro control. The modified coaxial .30 caliber gun is shown with its brass charging handle, shell collection chute and bag.

Scratch-built items include the 37mm gun guard and shell collection bag, and the left and right sides of the gun cradle. The modified antenna mount is shown to the right.

The breech ring for the 37mm gun was made up from styrene laminations carved and sanded to shape, and has an operating sliding breechblock. A .30 caliber ammo box from Dragon's Browning M1919A4 machine gun kit was used for the coaxial machine gun, and a turret manual traverse panel was made up from sheet and rod styrene and brass. The coaxial machine gun receiver is a cast metal one from Dragon in Dream and was converted from an M1919A4 to an A5 model by adding an extension to the charging handle and a firing solenoid under the trigger. It was further detailed with bolts, screws, and a shell ejection chute with collection bag. The 37mm gun gyro control was laminated up from sheet styrene. I've used various thicknesses for making up laminated components: .060", .080", .100", and .120". The gyro control is mounted on a shaft made from brass tubing. Using these techniques and the materials previously described I made up the guard for the 37mm gun, which includes a shell collection bag, and the left side of the gun cradle, including the gunner's telescopic sight. The face shield for the telescope was vacuum-formed over a pair of 1/6 scale goggles from a tanker figure. The right side of the gun cradle includes the mount for the .30 caliber coaxial gun with retaining pin and chain, and an electrical control box. The SCR-508 antenna was made from brass rod, with sections of steel hypodermic tubing representing the connectors for the three sections of antenna. The MP-48-A antenna base is from Armorpax and has a working spring flex mount. This item was detailed with brass bolts, styrene clamps, and wiring to make it the functional antenna for the radio control system, and it replaced the kit's unauthentic vinyl antenna.

The kit's non-scale 37mm gun barrel was replaced with a two-section Schumo-Kit™ aluminum barrel and sleigh that were to scale. The barrel had 12 grooves of rifling inserted made from Evergreen .010" x .020" strip styrene in a right-hand twist. The kit's firing servo was converted to an elevation servo for the barrel using a cam made from brass tubing. The gun mantlet was modified with a relocated .30 caliber machine gun opening, a brass visor over the gunner's telescope opening, revised contours, and hardware items, such as a socket screw under the barrel and two socket screws under the bottom of the mantlet. The circular plate representing the front opening of the turret behind the mantlet was highly modified to replicate the original. This involved changing the contours with sheet styrene and Milliput, enlarging and reshaping the opening for the 37mm gun and the .30 caliber coaxial machine gun, making an opening for the gunner's telescopic sight, filling unauthentic holes with styrene plugs, and creating a bead around all openings using .010" styrene rod. Small weld beads were done with 3M Acryl Green body putty.

The aluminum 37mm gun barrel has 12 rifling grooves (in a right-hand twist, of course!) made of strip styrene. The modified mantlet and turret front now appear as the full-size items did.

The turret hatches have resin hinges which replace the kit's toy-like ones. The brass locking handles and latching mechanisms operate as the originals did.

A view of the right side of the turret interior showing the mix of materials used in its construction and their placement.

Turret hatches

The turret hatches required some reshaping with strip styrene to fit properly and eliminate unsightly gaps between them and the turret roof. The four molded-on unauthentic hinges were cut and sanded away and were replaced with resin ones purchased separately from Panzerwerk. These were originally hinges for the engine hatch, so they had to be moderately reshaped. They have foundry casting numbers added, along with Milliput weld beads. The kit's oversize hatch handles on the outside were deleted, and were replaced with scale handles on the outside and inside from Armorpax. Closing and latching handles were fashioned from brass rod and were mounted inside the hatches using brass hardware attaching them to styrene housings. The handles operate as the originals did, and actually activate sliding bars which engage the external slots in the hatch rest mounts on the turret roof. The housings have foundry casting numbers added and are surrounded by Milliput weld beads. The handles snap into clamps made of brass sheet when stowed. Unauthentic holes from the deleted handles were filled with Milliput, and sheet styrene filled the gap left by cutting off the plain commander's closed periscope cover. The tank commander's hatch was modified to accept a Panzerwerk resin periscope that swivels 360 degrees. The Armorpax turret hatch kit also supplied the cast metal head pads seen in the photos. Brass sheet was used to make the clamps which the turret locking handles inside the turret engage when the hatches are closed. A padlock hasp made of styrene was added to the gunner's hatch forward edge.

The left side of the turret shows the gunner's sighting periscope, hatch locking handles, and the mix of materials detailing the periphery of the hatch openings.

Turret interior right sidewall

The turret had several thick reinforcing webs inside which had to be cut and ground away to create the room needed to detail the interior. Once this was done various stowage containers were added for grenades, the .45 caliber ammunition, and a spare periscope. These were made from .010" brass sheet soldered with Stay-Brite silver solder. The latches and locks on these containers were made up from sheet brass, styrene, and rod. Various hooks for headsets and wiring clamps were fashioned from brass sheet, along with an instruction panel. The four handles at the forward edge of the turret hatch openings used for locking the two hatches closed were made from brass tubing, sheet brass, and styrene, and have brass hardware hinges. Their closing springs are annealed brass wire wound around a mandrel to create a coil spring. The hatch openings were detailed with strip styrene around their edges, and the two hatch openings were divided with a longitudinal beam made from two sections of brass U-channel profiles. Two head pads were made from laminated sheet styrene and were installed on the front edges of the hatch openings.

Turret interior left sidewall

Several hooks for headsets and wiring clamps were made from brass sheet and styrene, along with a two-pronged clamp for a data folder on the rear sidewall. The gunner's sighting periscope was made up from sheet styrene and includes the face pad, mount, and scope, and brass rod was used to make the rod end for the link connecting the scope to the 37mm gun. A rack for the .30 caliber ammunition can was made from sheet styrene. Much of the interior molded-on reinforcing was cut away to make room for the 37mm gun breech.

The rear plate of the turret illustrating the antenna mount and base, grouser racks, and the modified plate allowing the 37mm gun to be removed through this opening on the real tank.

Turret exterior rear plate

The plate on the aft side of the turret exterior was highly modified. The lower section was cut away from the lower turret half and cemented to the upper turret half. The seam was filled with strip styrene and Milliput. The rectangular holes left when the unauthentic grouser blocks were deleted were filled with sheet styrene. The opening for removing the 37mm gun was edged with .010" x .060" brass strip around its perimeter to act as a dam for the weld bead made of Milliput. The armor plate panel covering the opening for removing the 37mm gun was stripped of unauthentic details and its undersize antenna mount, and had its edges beveled to an accurate contour. Four holes were drilled in its corners for brass bolts. A new antenna mount was made from sheet brass and styrene and has foundry casting numbers from the Lion Roar photoetch sheets. Small weld beads were made from 3M Acryl Green putty. The MP-48-A antenna base was threaded to accept a nut, star washer, and flat washer which secure it to the antenna mount. The wire leading from the antenna base into the turret connects to the radio control gear, making the scale antenna a functional one. Eight grouser mounting plates were made from brass angle and have holes drilled in them for mounting the grousers.

A Dremel Moto-tool with an oblong cutting bur make quick work of removing toy-like and unauthentic detail. A bit messy, perhaps, but effective. Doesn't smell very nice, either.

Turret roof exterior

Much of the molded-on turret detail was ground off and replaced. My preferred method was to use a round bur in my Dremel Moto-tool to remove most of the item. The Dremel was plugged into a Dremel speed control (rheostat) to slow down the tool to avoid melting the plastic. This is not a clean operation, nor does it smell very nice. But it goes quickly, and when the item is almost flush with the surface of the turret roof I use coarse, medium, and fine grit sanding sticks to polish out the area. The turret roof was then ready for me to add my own to-scale detail.

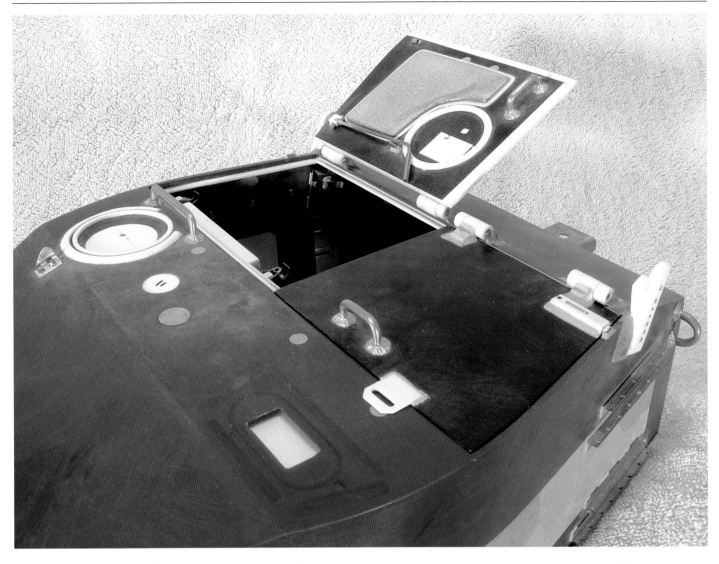

More items are added to the turret roof exterior including hatch rests, commander's vane sight, grab handles, and padlock hasp.

The area where the gunner's sighting periscope and armored wings were removed is polished and ready to receive my own scratch-built to-scale version of these items. A vane sight for the tank commander was made from .010" brass sheet and was bolted down in front of his periscope with brass 00-90 bolts. The kit's non-scale grab handles were replaced with cast metal Armorpax handles which were relocated to the proper location on the turret roof. A number of holes then had to be filled with styrene plugs.

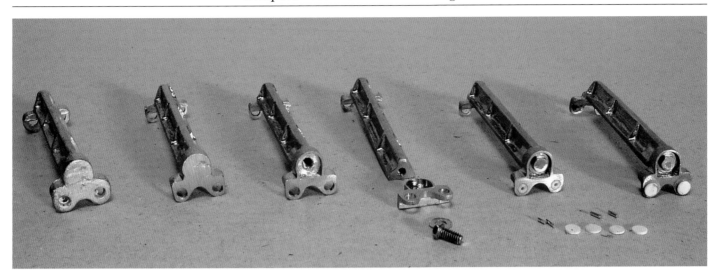

Six stages in detailing Armorpax cast metal grousers to make them operate and bolt up to their racks like the originals.

Detailing the grousers

Grousers were devices designed to increase the traction of the tracks in soft ground, mud, snow, or ice. They were carried on external turret racks when not needed and bolted on to every sixth track end connector when required. The kit's poorly-molded plastic grousers were removed and were replaced with cast metal ones from Armorpax, which have a much better appearance. As nice as these were, I found their detail could be enhanced and further, they could be made to operate just like the originals did. Photo 169 illustrates a six-step process I used to do this, from left to right in the photo.

1. The basic grouser casting as it comes from Armorpax.
2. The casting cleaned up: the ends sanded smooth with sanding sticks, flash cleaned off, seams eliminated, holes cleared of flash, and the external contours around the holes were filed down to make the grouser ends much thinner and more scale-like.
3. A socket for the bolt was created in the detachable end of the grouser by drilling and using burs, files, a sharp hobby knife, and sanding sticks. A tap hole was drilled in the socket for a 2-56 brass bolt, and then it was threaded with the proper tap.

4. The detachable end was sawn off using an X-ACTO razor saw with fine teeth. The raw ends were then polished smooth with several grades of sanding sticks.
5. Styrene rod was used to fill the four oversize holes in the grouser ends. These were cemented in place with CA (cyanoacrylate) glue, and when dry they were sanded flush with the metal. They were then drilled to accept four pins made of .025" brass rod.
6. Disks were punched out of .005" sheet styrene with my Waldron Punch & Die Set, and were used to cover the four holes in the ends of the grousers. Using CA glue generously caused these to appear as weld beads as per the originals.

Foundry casting numbers taken from the Lion Roar photoetch sheets were added to each grouser. This became somewhat tedious since there were 30 grousers to do, each with eight numbers. That's a total of 240 photoetch numbers to add one at a time. I can't believe I ended up doing this. I often wonder if therapy might help. There are actually spaces for 32 grousers on the external racks, but I left two off for a more candid appearance. At this point I didn't think I could do one more grouser....

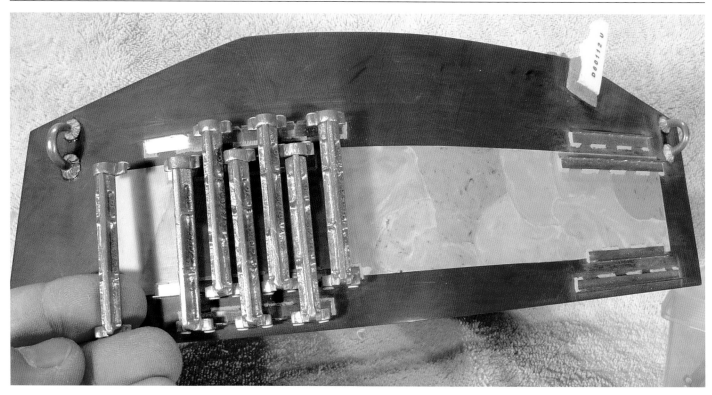

The grousers being bolted to their racks. The strip of Milliput putty fills the depression left by the removal of the plastic grouser strip from the model.

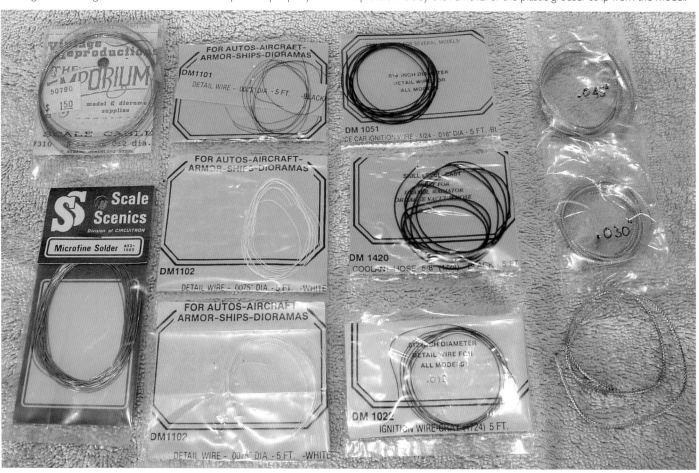

Several types of modeling wire used for scale wiring in the turret interior. Metal braided wiring conduit by Detail Master in three sizes is on the right.

When the strip of plastic grousers was removed from the left side of the turret it left a large rectangular depression which needed to be filled. This can be done with sheet styrene and CA glue or, as I did it, filling it a bit at a time with leftover Milliput whenever I used it elsewhere. Either method will do the job. The grouser racks were made from brass angle cut into sections to fit with each section drilled for each grouser's pins. The grousers are installed by fitting them to a rack, then tightening the grouser bolt to secure the grouser in place. I did the extra work to convert the grousers into operating ones like the originals for two reasons: one was simply the challenge of doing it; the other was that this allowed me to paint the grousers separately from the turret, then bolting them up in place at a later time. Weld beads were added to the grouser racks using 3M Acryl Green putty. The kit lacked the four turret lifting rings which were, in this case, supplied by Armorpax. The two hatch rest mounts were fashioned from laminated sheet styrene and include foundry casting numbers taken from the Lion Roar photoetch sheets. Weld beads were made from Milliput. These rests support the turret hatches when in the open position and have slots that the latches in the hatches engage to lock them in the open position.

Turret wiring

All of the functional wiring for the radio control system was done using small-gauge model railroad hook-up wire in red (positive) and black (negative). I used small strips of masking tape to label every wire and connection, since this made it simple to identify what wire went to where after much time had gone by and I had forgotten much of this. A variety of wire was used for the scale non-functional wiring in the turret, including Detail Master™ model car wiring using black and white in various diameters, which is very malleable and easy to form around bends. Detail Master also makes realistic braided metal wire conduit, which the full-size Stuart turret is filled with. I found three diameters most

useful and in scale for this project: .030", .045", and .060". Scale Scenics™ makes Microfine Solder,™ which is useful for creating hydraulic and oil lines, and which possesses the same malleability and ease of forming the Detail Master wire does.

Painting of interior turret components

The detail painting and assembly of the various interior components of the turret was one of the most enjoyable stages in the entire building process for me. Here the builder watches the interior come alive with color and things appear more realistic. The assembly of minor fittings and items and installing the scale wiring and braided electrical conduit lines makes one feel that real progress is being made. It's really satisfying to see it all come together, made more enjoyable by the fact that the process seems to happen quickly compared to basic construction. Three different 37mm rounds and an empty shell case from Panzerwerk were painted by first airbrushing the projectile portion of the rounds. The M2 Canister and the M74 armor-piercing projectiles were painted flat black, while the M51 armor-piercing capped round was painted medium blue. The stenciling on these was made up by applying white dry transfer lettering to clear decal paper, then overcoating with Testors Dullcote to fix the letters in place. These markings were then applied to the projectiles as wet transfers. The brass shell cases were airbrushed with SnJ Spray Metal™. This is an excellent paint and powder system which replicates real metal. It does this well since it *is* real metal. I first airbrushed the shell cases with SnJ Bronze paint. When this was dry I used a cotton swab to apply a mixture of SnJ Aluminum and Bronze metal powder to duplicate the color and sheen of brass. This can be immediately buffed out with the polishing cloth included in the SnJ kit, and the result is spectacularly real. Other painted items include the 37mm gun control box, the power traverse handle and box, and the manual traverse unit with a holder for a pair of binoculars. The placard reading "BINOCULARS" outlined in black was made up on the

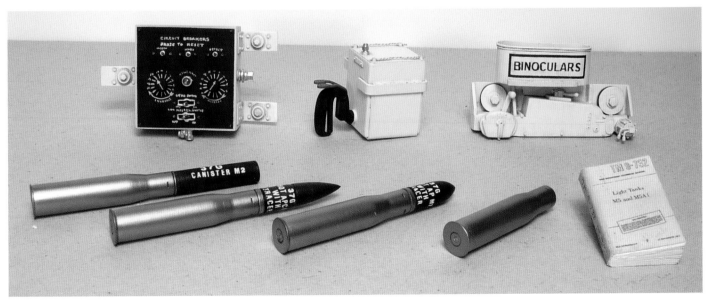

A line-up of some items for the turret interior: three different 37mm rounds and an empty shell case from Panzerwerk. In the rear are several scratch-built items: the 37mm gun control box, the power traverse handle and box, the manual traverse unit with binocular holder, and a 1/6 scale copy of technical manual TM 9-732 for the M5 and M5A1.

The right side of the scratch-built 37mm gun cradle with breech ring, recoil guard, gunner's telescope, and co-axial M1919A5 .30 caliber machine gun.

computer using the program Paint, then printing this–and many other turret interior placards–on clear decal paper using an inkjet printer. After allowing them to dry overnight I lightly oversprayed the placards with Testors Dullcote to fix the lettering in place. Once dry these were applied as wet transfers. A 1/6 scale copy of technical manual TM 9-732 for the M5 and M5A1 was made by scanning the full-size original, reducing it on the computer to 1/6 scale, then printing it on manila card. The pages within are blank and were made up from scrap printer paper. I know that somewhere, sometime, some contest judge will open this manual with his probe and will discover it's blank. I, of course, will lose points because of this. Having been a judge myself upon occasion I know it's inevitable...sigh.

The 37mm gun cradle and recoil guard was airbrushed Olive Drab, which I mixed myself from Floquil's Roof Brown, Depot Olive, and Reefer Yellow.

The 37mm gun breech ring, breech block, gunner's telescope mounting bracket, and the M1919A5 .30 caliber coaxial machine gun were airbrushed to represent a Parkerized finish using Floquil Engine Black, Old Silver, and Reefer Gray. When dry these items were polished with graphite powder taken from a draftsman's pencil sharpener, which gave them a realistic metallic sheen. The gun cradle assembly was then weathered using pin washes and pastels, and it exhibits minor chipping.

The left side of the gun cradle, breech ring, silver firing solenoid, and recoil guard with cloth shell case collection bag.

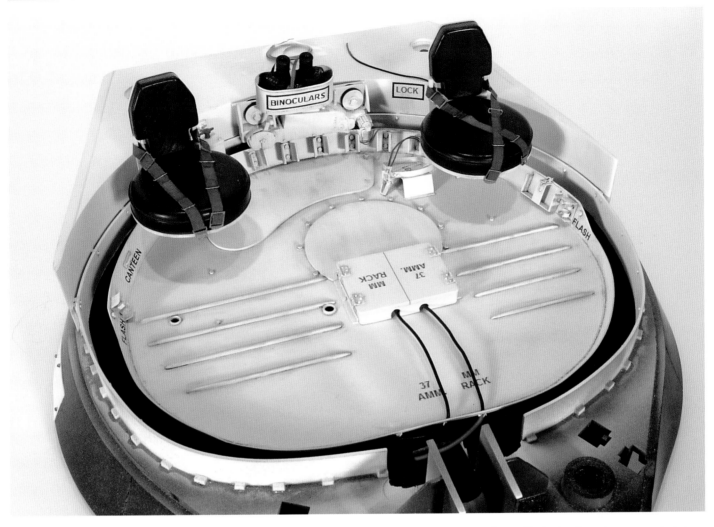

The scratch-built turret basket with seats and belts, shell holders, flashlight brackets, and spotlight stowage fixture. The basket floor does not project down into the hull a scale distance due to the underlying radio control components located there, but this will be much less noticeable when viewed through the hatches when the turret is finished.

The turret interior and basket were airbrushed Floquil Reefer White darkened with a touch of Reefer Gray. The seat cushions were painted Floquil Engine Black, which was allowed to cure for several days before lightly rubbing them with a trace of hand lotion to give them the soft sheen of leather. The seat belts were made up from strips cut from tightly-woven muslin fabric which were airbrushed faded Olive Drab and fitted with photoetch buckles and loops from a Lion Roar photoetch sheet for 1/6 scale figures. The interior was given some pin washes and applications of pastels to create the wear and tear so common to the inside of a turret which has seen extensive use in combat. The turret basket does not project down into the hull a scale distance due to the radio control components located underneath it, but this will be much less noticeable when it's viewed through the hatches after the turret is finished. There is so much detail and equipment inside the turret that the eye does not readily see past this to notice the shallowness of the basket floor. I'm not entirely happy with this non-scale fact, but it was necessary to preserve the R/C functions of the model without major modifications. In any event, this was one of the several compromises I had to agonize over during the course of the build. My excuse is that nothing built by the human hand is perfect, regardless of the builder's best intentions, and I've found that I'm very human...sigh.

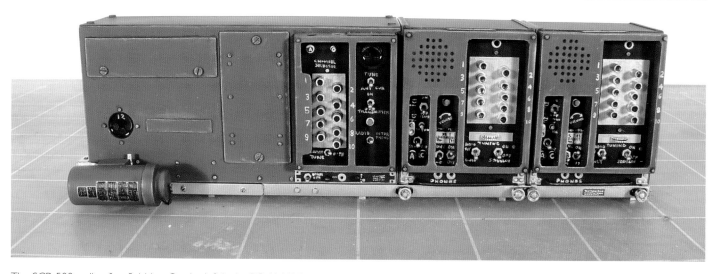

The SCR-508 radio after finishing. On the left is the BC-604 FM transmitter; in the middle and on the right are two BC-603 FM receivers. These sit on a FT-237 Mounting which has an A-62 Phantom Antenna (the cylindrical object) screwed on the left.

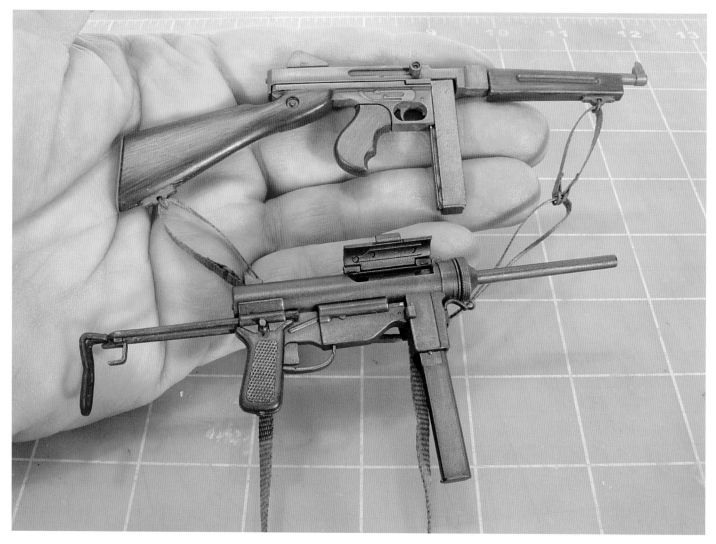

A Thompson M1928A1 .45 caliber submachine gun which will be stowed on top of the SCR-508 radio. The metal parts on this and the M3 .45 caliber submachine gun were painted in a Parkerized finish made from flat black, silver, and flat gray. The wooden parts are painted a light tan base coat with raw umber oil paint streaked on for wood grain.

The SCR-508 radio was airbrushed Olive Drab and all details were hand-painted, then lightly weathered with a silver Prismacolor artist's pencil. The silver was feathered out and made less distinct using a Colour Shaper tool. The "glass" over the several dials and meters was made with clear gloss. The BC-604 FM transmitter is on the left; in the middle and on the right are two BC-603 FM receivers. These sit on a FT-237 mounting which has an A-62 phantom antenna (the cylindrical object) screwed on the left. Several black and silver data plates from Archer Fine Transfers (truck data plates) were added.

A Thompson M1928A1 .45 caliber submachine gun from Dragon will later be stowed on top of the SCR-508 radio. The metal parts on this were painted in a Parkerized finish made from flat black, silver, and flat gray. The wooden parts were painted with a light tan base coat which was allowed to dry thoroughly. Then raw umber oil paint was streaked on to produce the wood grain. The canvas straps on this weapon were painted a thinned mixture of Olive Drab for both penetration and slight changes in tonal appearance.

Turret exterior

A pyrogravure was used to create the flame-cut edges to the turret side armor plates. This is nothing more than a soldering iron with a blade tip, and it was plugged into a rheostat to turn down the temperature of the iron. By practicing on scrap plastic I found the ideal heat to create the lined edges without rapidly melting the plastic. Just enough heat to score the closely-spaced lines is best. Numerous weld beads were made by the usual method of Milliput putty sculpted over an engraved line cut along the weld bead areas to help the putty adhere better.

A pyrogravure (soldering iron with a blade tip) was used to create the flame-cut edges to the turret armor side plates. The larger weld beads were made with Milliput epoxy putty.

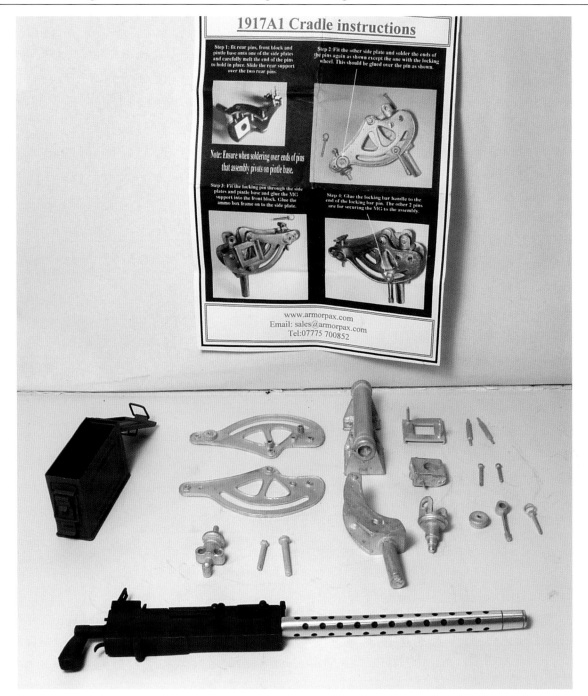

The .30 caliber M1919A4 Browning anti-aircraft machine gun is comprised of the Armorpax mount and cradle kits, plus DiD's brass barrel and ammo box. The black DiD gun receiver was replaced with the more highly detailed plastic Dragon M1919A4.

To model a mid-production M5A1 I would have to cut off the armor shield around the anti-aircraft machine gun on the right side of the turret, then sand and fill any traces of its outline. The Armorpax cast-metal kits of the machine gun mount and the gun cradle would be the starting points for creating the exposed .30 caliber gun. I had planned to use the DiD Browning M1919A4 machine gun, but later replaced the metal receiver with the one from the plastic Dragon kit, since it was more accurate and had better detail. The DiD barrel was kept, since it was brass and of a scale thinness compared to the plastic Dragon barrel.

The turret left side shows the strip where the removal of the kit's unauthentic grousers was filled with Milliput, plus the new brass angle grouser racks, weld seams, and other details.

The turret's left side had the kit's unauthentic rubbery plastic grouser strip removed, which left a long recess in the armor plate. This was filled bit by bit with Milliput left over from other steps requiring this putty, thus not wasting this excess. New grouser racks were made up from brass angle strip, and the grousers are attached to these as per the prototype: by fitting the grouser to the top and bottom angle, then tightening the grouser bolt to clamp the grouser in place.

The turret skirt was modified in the rear to maintain the continuous outward flare around its circumference, rather than being vertical as molded in the kit. Scale bolts, nuts, and washers were added under the turret bustle to duplicate the hardware attaching the radio mount inside. Other details were added, such as grouser racks, the radio antenna mount, weld beads, and four turret lift rings from Armorpax.

The turret rear view shows brass grouser racks, radio antenna mount, hardware, weld beads, and how the turret skirt was modified in the rear to maintain the continuous outward flare around its circumference.

The turret right side view shows brass angle grouser racks and weld beads. The Armorpax machine gun mount and cradle were modified with scale hardware so all adjustments work as per the original.

The turret front view shows the newly-formed opening around the barrel, gunner's telescope, casting marks and numbers, weld beads, Armorpax lifting rings, and the gunner's sighting periscope with a brush guard made from brass rod.

The turret right side received grouser racks and weld beads, plus an access panel in the turret skirt made from .015" brass sheet. This provided a means to access the turret bearings on the real item. The Armorpax M20 machine gun mount and cradle had all the cast-on bolt heads and nuts ground off. These were replaced with brass bolts, nuts, and washers of the appropriate size. Some lathe work produced additional fittings and handles which allow all the moving features of the cradle to work. This means the locking handle on the right can be rotated to loosen the cradle for large elevation adjustments, while precision adjustments are made with the two knurled wheels at the aft end for traverse and elevation. While this is primarily a static model, it was both challenging and fun to make it all work just like the full-size cradle. Don't ask me why.

The cover for the 37mm gun on the turret front plate was blended in with Milliput to appear as a single casting. The opening for the gun barrel was opened up to an accurate shape and has a raised bead made from styrene rod formed around the opening. Foundry casting numbers were obtained from the Kit Kraft plastic lettering kit. Four casting plug cut-offs made from styrene strip were added to the corners of the front plate. The gunner's sighting telescope opening was drilled out and the telescope was made from a length of brass tubing. Clear disks cut from acetate sheet became the lenses for this instrument.

The turret top plate received a gunner's sighting periscope which was modified from the Panzerwerk crew periscopes. This involved making a new base plate from sheet styrene, adding four brass flat head screws, and then protecting it with two armored guards and two bullet splash guards made from styrene sheet and strip. Further protection comes from a brush guard soldered up from brass rod. Smaller details include grab handles from Armorpax, a brass lock from 6th Scale Icons™, and a brass sighting vane formed from brass sheet in front of the commander's periscope. The turret hatches will lock in the open position using the handles just as in the original.

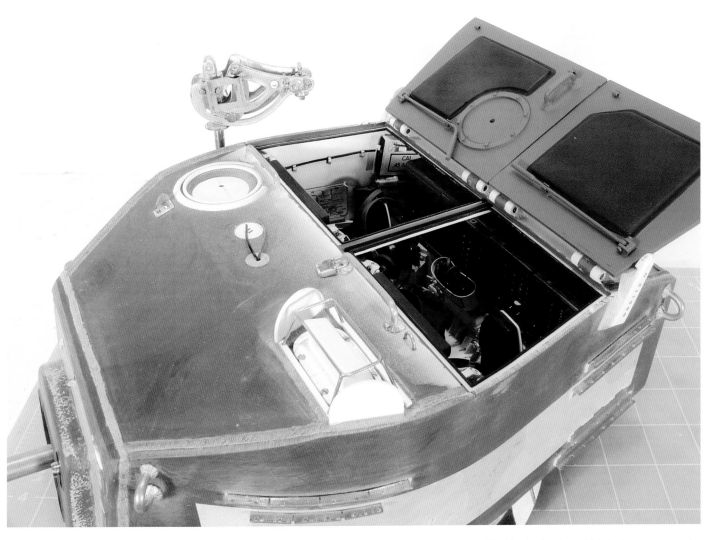

The turret top view shows the gunner's sighting periscope and brush guard, weld beads, and interior detail inside the hatches which lock open as per the original.

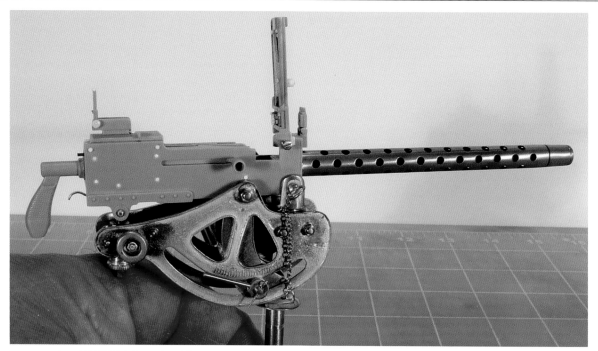

The completed M1919A4 Browning .30 caliber machine gun is comprised of a Dragon receiver, a DiD barrel, and an Armorpax cradle. The cradle was made fully functional with scale hardware and adjusting knobs. The weapon's bolt is spring-loaded and the top plate swivels.

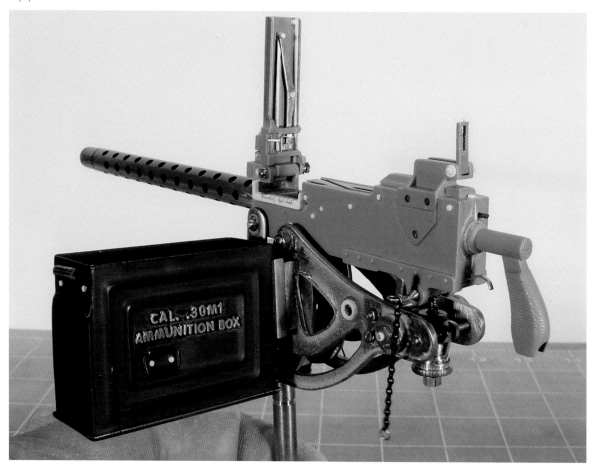

The unit was extensively modified with styrene and brass & steel hardware to make the cradle functional in coarse elevation, plus fine elevation and traverse adjustments. The ammo box is a modified DiD item which clips into the cradle and is labeled with Lion Roar brass letters.

The M1919A4 Browning .30 caliber machine gun is comprised of a Dragon receiver, a DiD barrel, and an Armorpax cradle. The cradle needed to be cleaned of flash and molding seams, which was easily done with files and sanding sticks. It was made fully functional with scale nuts, bolts, spacers, washers, adjusting knobs, and a locking handle turned from brass rod on the lathe. These new brass items had a better appearance than the kit items, which were molded a bit out of round. The weapon's bolt works and is driven to the closed position by a spring made from brass wire wound around a mandrel. The top plate opens and locks the ammo belt in place when closed. Model ship chains prevent the loss of the two pins that hold the weapon in place in the cradle.

The gun and cradle unit was extensively modified and detailed with styrene, brass, and steel hardware to make the cradle functional in coarse elevation, plus fine elevation and traverse vernier adjustments. Pulling the fore and aft mounting pins will allow the gun to be dismounted from the cradle. The gun's top plate was detailed with the ammunition feed, extraction, and ejection mechanism, all made from brass sheet and rod. The ammo box is a modified DiD item which clips into the cradle and is labeled with Lion Roar brass letters.

The spotlight and its mount had to be entirely scratch-built; an interesting project, since I had not done any machining of this nature previously. It was both challenging and fun to make all the items in this assembly, learning as I went. The mount for the spotlight was turned on a Sherline lathe from 1-inch diameter brass rod which I procured from MetalsDepot®, an online metals supplier. It came in a 1-foot length and seemed somewhat expensive at $30.00 plus shipping, but I was able to make everything I needed from this one piece: the spotlight, shield, and mount. It was also used to make the four mounts for the track return rollers and several other items, so it was money well spent. The mount attaches to the turret roof with four oval-head 00-80 screws. I turned down four flat-head screws on the lathe to make the correct oval-head types, a simple operation. The mount is surrounded by a bullet splash guard made from bent .040" x .040" brass strip. The rain cap used to keep water out of the mount when the light is stowed in the turret was also turned on the lathe, as was the small cap mount used to secure the rain cap to the turret roof when the spotlight is mounted. Some model ship chain was used to secure the rain cap to the mount. I gently squeezed each round link in the chain to make it more oval-shaped to conform to photos of the real thing. The chain is attached on each end with S-hooks bent up from brass rod. 3M Acryl Green body putty was used for the three weld beads.

The mount for the spotlight was turned on a Sherline lathe from brass rod. It screws to the turret roof and is surrounded by a brass strip bullet splash guard. The mount cap, chain, and cap retainer mount were also turned on the lathe. 3M Acryl Green body putty was used for weld beads. The brass padlock for the gunner's hatch is a 6th Scale Icons photoetch brass kit.

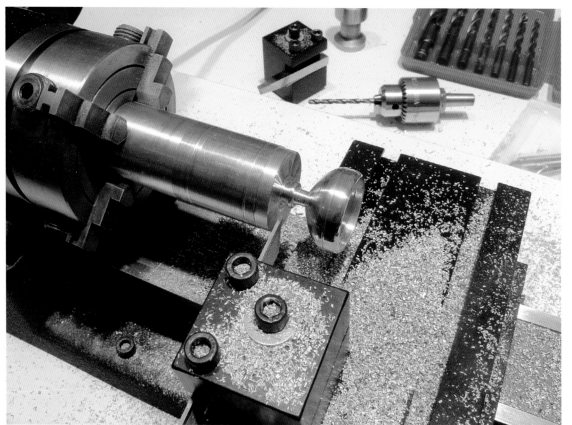

The Sherline lathe turning the spotlight out of 1" diameter solid brass rod. A four-jaw chuck was necessary to hold the brass rod securely enough due to the weight of the brass and the forces involved. A parting tool is being used to cut the spotlight's knob.

Below: The components of the scratch-built spotlight: the mounting handle, the light housing, the shield, a bright white LED, a reflector cut from a small flashlight, and a clear vacuum-formed lens. The spotlight is wired into the headlight lighting circuit.

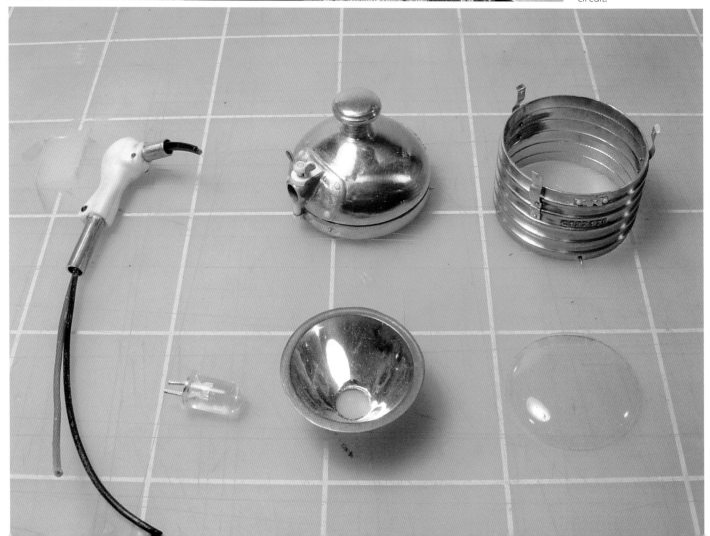

I used my Sherline lathe to turn the spotlight out of 1-inch diameter solid brass rod. At first I used the standard three-jaw chuck, but the brass bar flew partially out of the chuck with a heart-stopping noise. I tried using my Sherline Steady Rest attachment to stabilize the brass but to no effect; the same thing happened again. A bit of thought made me decide to install the optional four-jaw chuck, which would provide more support and clamping effect, and this turned out to be successful. The four-jaw chuck overcame the weight of the brass stock and the cutting forces involved and proved to be the answer. I used a combination of a left- and a right-hand cutting tool, as well as a parting tool, to form out the spotlight, its knob on the back end, and the shield. The lathe's drill chuck, holding a centering drill, was used to start the hole in the interior of the light and the shield, and a standard drill and a boring tool were used to bring the interior of the light and the shield to their final dimensions. Lathe work is not a clean operation, and a shop vacuum is a necessity. Making the scratch-built spotlight was a challenge but a fun one, and I learned much regarding various machining operations using a lathe. I'm a bit more confident now about taking on more complex projects using the lathe and its various accessories. Although I still consider myself somewhat of a beginner, I find myself improving in skill, accuracy, and proper machining methods each time I tackle a new lathe project.

The spotlight sits on a mounting handle which has two sections of soldered-together brass tubing at its core, and two sections of sheet styrene were used sandwich-fashion to make up the handle. Various details were added to the handle, spotlight, and shield from styrene and brass rod and sheet. A bright white LED fits into a reflector modified from a small flashlight and is wired into the headlight/taillight circuit. A clear lens was vacuum-formed over a shaped styrene disk and was installed with diluted white glue.

The various casting and Ordnance Department drawing numbers evident on the components of the light are photoetch letters and numbers from the Lion Roar sheets. The assembled spotlight is comprised of some 87 parts.

The assembled spotlight with the shield clipped onto it. The name of the original manufacturer (GUIDE) is made from brass photoetch letters. There are 87 parts in this assembly.

The Ordnance drawing numbers are brass photoetch letters & numbers from Lion Roar. The three spring clips on the shield work like the originals to clip the shield to the lamp housing which makes it removable.

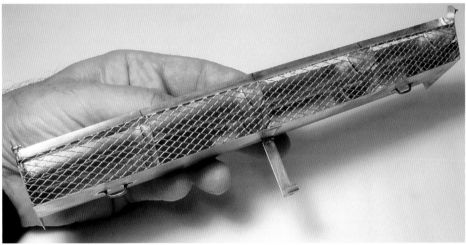

The upper air deflector was soldered up from .015" sheet brass, including the securing strap and hinge on the bottom. The screening is 1/4" pattern Copperform Mesh from AMACO.

The upper air deflector is essentially a unit comprised of three vanes or baffles which turn the warm air exhausting from the engine compartment 90 degrees from straight down to straight aft. This eliminated the dust cloud the tank raised which helped to conceal its position.

There is still a certain amount of hand work when using a lathe, such as applying small files to rotating parts to smooth edges, create round profiles, scoring thin lines, and polishing out machining marks with sanding sticks. The three spring clips on the shield work like the originals to clip the shield to the lamp housing. This makes the shield removable; convenient for painting separately and showing off to friends. The front post sight was made from brass rod, while the rear notch sight was cut from brass sheet.

Upper air deflector

At this point it was deemed a good time to construct the upper air deflector described in Chapter 6. I waited until this point in the build since the deflector had to be made to fit the rear of the hull and this was now finished. The fitted deflector was then painted and put aside to avoid damage to it until it was needed during the final detailing phase of the model.

Working with stencils

1. Trim around the stencil just enough to allow it to fit in place. Remove the backing film to expose the adhesive and put the stencil in place on the model. Burnish down the edges to seal them, which eliminates paint bleeding beneath the stencil. This is done with a dry transfer burnishing tool found at an art store.

2. Peel away the top protective film, which maintains the shape of the stencil until it's firmly in place. Burnish down the edges a second time, since some may have lifted when peeling off the top protective layer.

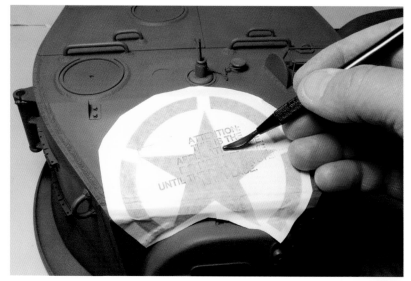

Working with stencils #1: Trim around the stencil just enough to allow it to fit in place. Remove the backing film to expose the adhesive and put the stencil in place. Burnish down the edges to seal them which eliminates paint bleeding beneath the edges of the stencil. This is done with a dry transfer burnishing tool found at an art store.

Working with stencils #2: Peel away the top protective film which maintains the shape of the stencil until it's firmly in place. Burnish down the edges a second time since some may have lifted when peeling off the top protective layer.

3. Use small strips of masking tape to protect more of the area around the stencil.
4. Airbrush on the desired color spraying from the edge of the stencil in towards the center to avoid forcing paint under the stencil's edge.
5. When the paint is thoroughly dry gently peel the stencil off the model. Some overspray and bleeding may be evident that will require touching up, especially around complex shapes, as seen here.

Working with stencils #3: Use small strips of masking tape to protect more of the area around the stencil from overspray.

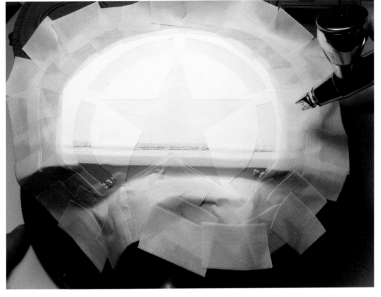

Working with stencils #4: Airbrush on the desired color spraying from the edge of the stencil in towards the center to avoid forcing paint under the stencil's edge.

Working with stencils #5: When the paint is thoroughly dry gently peel the stencil off the model. Some overspray and bleeding may be evident that will require touching up.

Working with stencils #6: Touch-up can be accomplished by very gentle scraping with a sharp hobby knife, light washing with paint thinner using a fine brush, and by dry brushing with the background color. Result: a perfect marking.

6. Touch-up can be accomplished by very gentle scraping with a sharp hobby knife, light washing with paint thinner using a fine brush, and by dry brushing with the background color. Result: a perfect marking.

13

Final Assembly

Adding the turret

At this point the turret was finished (for the most part) and lacked only final delicate detailing. Now was the time to attach the turret to the upper hull, since it had to be secured from inside. This was an awkward operation, because both the turret and upper hull were so large and heavy. The answer was to lay both on their side on a folded towel to protect the paint work, holding the turret in my left hand while my right was screwing down the turret retaining ring from within the lower hull. Once the turret was attached to the upper hull both these components were laid on edge alongside the lower hull to make all the final wiring connections. All electrical systems were tested for correct operation at this point, since there would be very limited access once the upper and lower hull sections were permanently joined. Basically this was my last chance to make sure everything was operating correctly.

When the turret's basic detailing was finished (but prior to final detailing) it was attached to the upper hull. The model was placed on a folded towel to protect the paint during attachment and the soldering of all the wiring between the turret and hull. Here two hands are attempting to attach the turret when three are required.

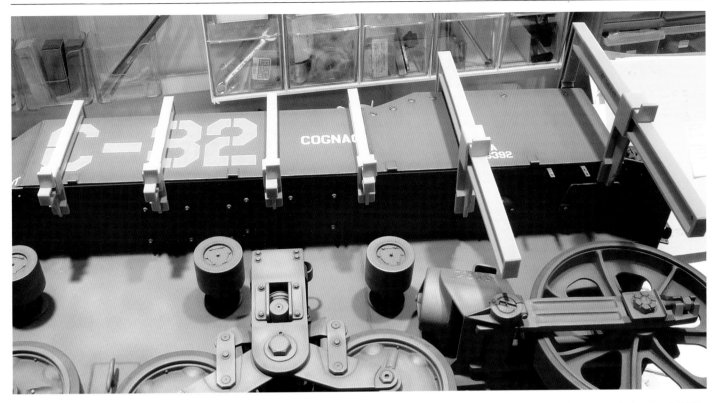

Lining up the upper and lower hull sections for gluing was made easy with the use of clamps (The tracks had to come off for this step). A strip of .040" x .040" styrene was necessary to fill the gap between the hull sections. CA glue was used for the bond.

Joining the upper and lower hulls

For the joining of the two hull sections the tracks would be in the way, so they had to come off temporarily. They were removed, carefully rolled up, then stored inside plastic bags until they were reinstalled on the tank. Satisfied with everything thus far, I gingerly slid the upper hull into position on the lower, then laid the complete tank on its side on the folded towel. Seven screws attached the upper hull to the lower from below through holes in the bottom plate of the hull. These holes had to be filled with circular plugs shaped from .060" sheet styrene which were cemented in place with CA glue. The plugs had then to be hidden by filling the seams with CA glue, sanding, texturing with Mr. Surfacer 500, and airbrushing Olive Drab. When dry, these locations were airbrushed with Dullcote to bring them into the same reflectance as the rest of the hull's bottom surface. They were now invisible. The full-size M5A1 upper and lower hulls were further joined by ten bolts on the lower edge of the glacis plate, which run width-wise. The recesses or sockets for these bolts may be seen in the photo on page 77. The preparation of these recesses was described Chapter 10, "Stage 3-Glacis Plate". The two outboard bolts on each side screw into

drilled and tapped holes in the final drive housings. The middle six bolts protrude down through the glacis plate and through the lip on the forward edge of the lower hull. Underneath this lip, these bolts are captured by nuts riding over flat washers, and these are very visible if you care to look under there. I used 1/2-inch 2-56 brass bolts for these, cut to length and with the ends ground to a cone-shaped tip. The sides of the upper hull join to the lower hull sides inside the lower edge of the sponsons, and here we have a problem with a large gap. Fortunately this gap lies right along the real tank's longitudinal weld bead under the sponsons. This was filled with .040" x .040" strip styrene at the time of gluing using CA cement. I made certain this strip was slightly recessed below the hull joining surfaces, since I would later hide this seam with a weld bead made of Milliput, and this slight recess would give the putty more gripping surface. Large and small clamps by X-ACTO were used to bring the edges of the hull joining surfaces into alignment for gluing. I glued one side up, let it sit overnight, then flipped the tank over onto its other side to complete the joining. I was careful not to apply glue in the vicinity of the clamps until they were removed so that they did not become part of the completed model, a horrible thought.

When the CA glue had dried thoroughly a weld bead of terra cotta-colored Milliput was used to fill the seam. The home-made weld bead tool had its jaws spread a bit more to make a full-width impression on this wide weld bead. The white dot left of the bogie is one of the hull attaching screw holes filled with a styrene disk.

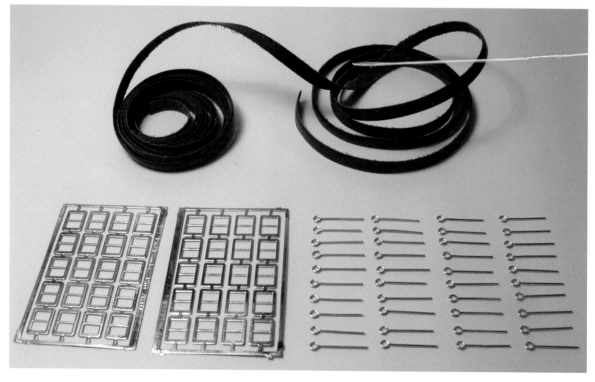

Making tie-down straps #1: The 3/16" leather strip, photoetch buckles, and prongs, or tongues, as they come from Rio Rondo.

I used terra-cotta colored Milliput (Just for variety. Okay, after several years of nothing but *tank* I was ready for some variety) to make the fore and aft weld beads under the sponsons. These weld beads conveniently hide the seams between the upper and lower hull sections, which makes eliminating them a lot easier. These weld beads are wider than previous ones, so I spread the jaws of my weld bead-making tool (last seen in the top photo on page 93) a bit further apart so that the impressions it would make would cover the entire width of the bead. When the Milliput had dried overnight, I masked off these areas and used my airbrush to cover them with Olive Drab paint. A final overcoat with Dullcote to blend everything together and this seam operation was done.

Making tie-down straps

All of the tools and stowage items were secured to the actual vehicle with leather tie-down straps. I found a nice source for materials to make these straps at Rio Rondo Enterprises™, a supplier for the model horse trade. I chose 3/16" wide straps for a proper size in 1/6 scale and found these to be ideal: supple, easily worked, and made of a nice grade of kangaroo leather. Kangaroo leather?!

1. The 3/16" leather strip, photoetch buckles, and tongues, or prongs, as they come from Rio Rondo are nice for the large scale model horses they're intended for, but require modification to become tool and equipment tie-down straps for an American tank of World War II.

2. The double buckle is clipped almost in half using cutters to form a single frame, then it is ground and filed to a more rounded shape using photos for reference. The straps are cut to a 2 1/2" actual length. When finished the straps will be a scale 14" long, including the buckle. A number of straps will of necessity have to be longer to span the distance between their footman or tie-down loops, and these are best measured by laying them on the model to determine their proper length.

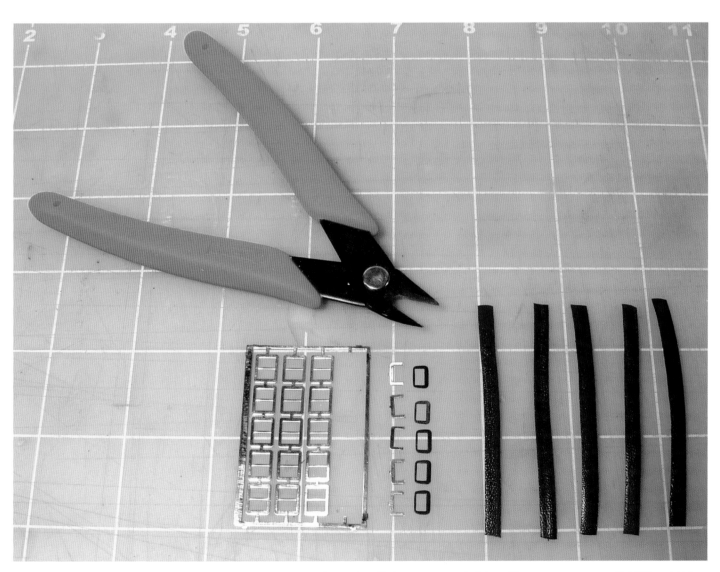

Making tie-down straps #2: The double buckle is clipped to a single frame, then filed to more rounded shape. The straps are cut to a 2 1/2" length. When finished most straps will be a scale 14" long including the buckle.

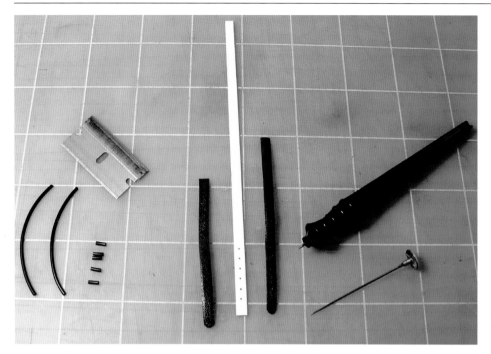

Making tie-down straps #3: Insulation with the wire removed is cut to length for placement on the buckles. A plastic template is made from styrene strip to punch equally-spaced holes in the straps.

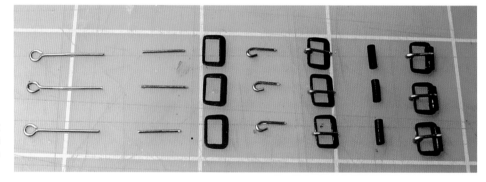

Making tie-down straps #4: The prongs are cut shorter, then bent around the buckle frames. The lengths of wire insulation are sliced and slid into place on the buckles.

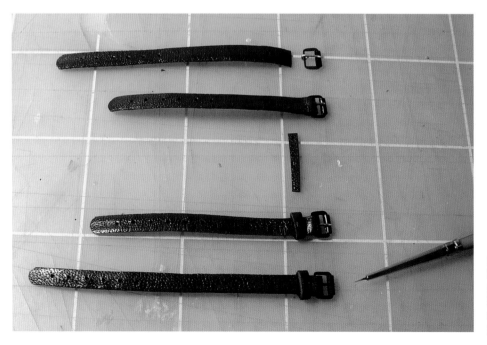

Making tie-down straps #5: A hole for the prong is punched in the strap, the buckle fitted into place, then the strap is glued around back to itself. A thin piece of leather is glued around the strap as a retainer loop. The hardware is then painted flat black.

3. Round wire insulation with the wire removed is cut to length for placement on the buckles. A plastic template is made from styrene strip to enable me to punch equally-spaced holes in the straps for the buckle prongs.

4. The prongs are cut shorter, then bent around the buckle frames. The lengths of wire insulation are sliced and slid into place on the buckles, then secured with CA glue.

5. A hole for the prong is punched in the strap and the buckle fitted into place; then the strap is glued around back to itself using CA glue. A thin piece of leather is glued around the strap as a retainer loop. The hardware is then painted flat black. After installation on the tank the satin finish of the straps is reduced by airbrushing each strap with Testors Dullcote for a more realistic reflectance.

Adding final details

Two M1936 field packs (Musette bags) from DiD were added to the engine deck, and were secured using the tie-down straps. The Musette bags were first weathered by brush-painting them with Olive Drab, which produced a realistic blotchy and irregular finish. They were further dirtied and muddied with pastels. A Berol Prismasolor Silver 949 pencil was used to create wear around the edges of the metal buckles on the packs and tie-down straps. This pencil deposits a wax-like silver substance on whatever surface you wish. Colour Shapers with five different tips were then used to blend the silver deposits in to a faded, indistinct, and realistic worn appearance.

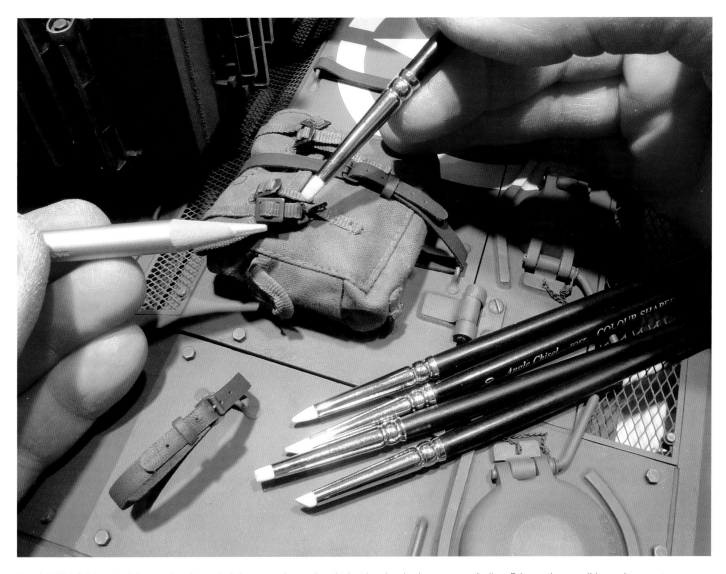

Two M1936 field packs (Musette bags) are tied down on the engine deck using the tie-down straps. A silver Prismasolor pencil is used to create wear on metal buckles and Colour Shapers with five different tips are used to blend the waxy silver deposits in.

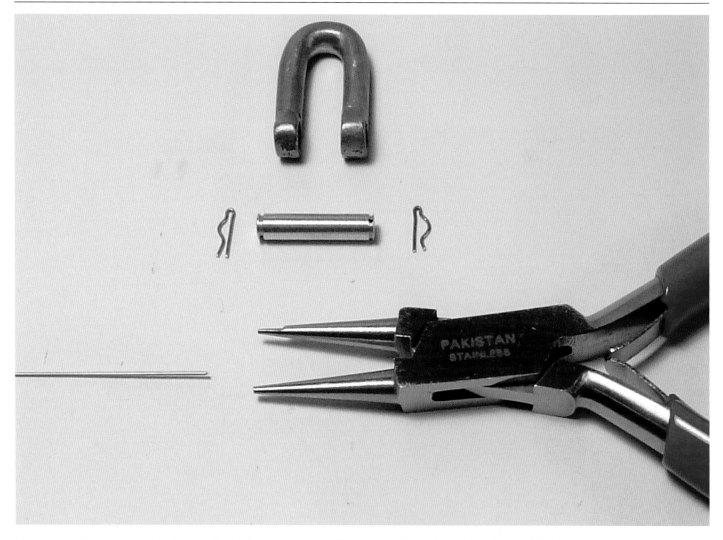

New shackle pins were turned on the lathe for the Armorpax shackles. Grooves were formed on each end, holes drilled, and hitch pins were bent up from .019" brass rod using round-nose pliers.

The four Armorpax white metal shackles needed to have new shackle pins made that were more detailed and authentic than those provided. The new pins were easily turned from brass rod on the lathe, including the grooves around both ends of each pin. A .022" hole was drilled through each end of the pins centered on the grooves. The shackle pins were secured in place in the shackles with two hitch pins. These I bent up from .019" brass wire using round-nose pliers. To be able to bend brass wire around a smaller radius I ground one tip of the pliers down, as may be seen in the photo.

Finishing touches

The tow cable was airbrushed Olive Drab. When this was dry it was given a wash of flat black. After this had dried overnight I washed burnt umber oil paint into the weave of the cable to simulate rust. After several days of drying I then applied powdered graphite from the pencil sharpener to the exterior strands of the cable with Colour Shapers, which brought out the texture of the cable's strands beautifully. The cable was shackled up to the towing points

of the tank, two cable tie-down straps were installed, and minor touch-up work was done.

Some weathering was done with Doc O'Brien's Weathering Powders in various colors to simulate dust, dried mud, rust, wear, abrasions, and oil stains. Graphite powder was applied to all sharp edges of the hull, turret, and various components of the vehicle and suspension to simulate wear and tear. Anxious not to overdo it, at this point I called it finished and placed the tank in its Plexiglas case.

Final thoughts

So what was the final tally for this project? The time and labor turned out to be more than I initially thought when I first started. My somewhat official log shows the model consumed 2573 hours spread over four years and six months of time, and it has 10,960 parts and pieces in it. Yes, I kept track. I can't help it: it's something innate in me (sigh). But when I look at the model in its showcase and reflect on all the challenges presented to me during the course of this project and the great amount of fun I had, I come away with the feeling that I'd do it all again.

14

Gallery:
The M5A1 Stuart Light Tank in 1/6 Scale

A series of walk-around photographs present the finished 1/6 scale M5A1 Stuart light tank.

The finished model's right side. Floquil Mud and Dust were airbrushed to depict weathering while Doc O'Brien's weathering powders in various earth colors were lightly brushed on.

The sides of the lower and upper hull have more road dust and dirt than the turret, appropriate for dusty roads in Normandy during June 1944.

The headlights and spotlight are Bright White LEDs on a separate power switch. The spotlight swivels left and right and up and down like the original.

Burnt Umber oil paint was used to depict rust on the tow cable, cable ends, and shackles. Powdered graphite from my draftsman's pencil sharpener was used to highlight the outer strands of the cable, applied with Colour Shapers.

The tow cable is secured with clamps and tie-down straps as per the original.

Two grousers are missing from the forward turret grouser rack for a more candid appearance.

The spare track blocks and all the tools are removable, being secured by scale bolts, clamps, and tie-down straps which work like the originals.

A view of the upper and lower air deflectors and the baffles within them. The large wrench is used to adjust track tension and this system works on the model just as on the full-size tank.

The two metal brackets hanging down from under the rear sponson are attachment points for the dust skirts which have been removed, as per photos of the original.

The tripod for the bow gunner's (BOG) machine gun is secured with tie-down straps and sits protected behind a brush guard.

Controversy surrounds the device mounted on the hull in front of the gunner's .30 caliber machine gun. Many experts feel it is a bullet deflector designed to deflect .30 caliber rounds from the hull machine gun downwards. This would be important for keeping German heads down while the tank is hull-up crashing through a hedge row.

The drive sprockets were heavily modified as to the shape of the teeth, hardware, and details. The detail of the supporting structure under the brass fenders is visible.

The idler bracket containing the horizontal volute spring was made from a pill bottle. The idler wheel articulates up and down and is supported by the spring. The track tension is adjusted like the original was.

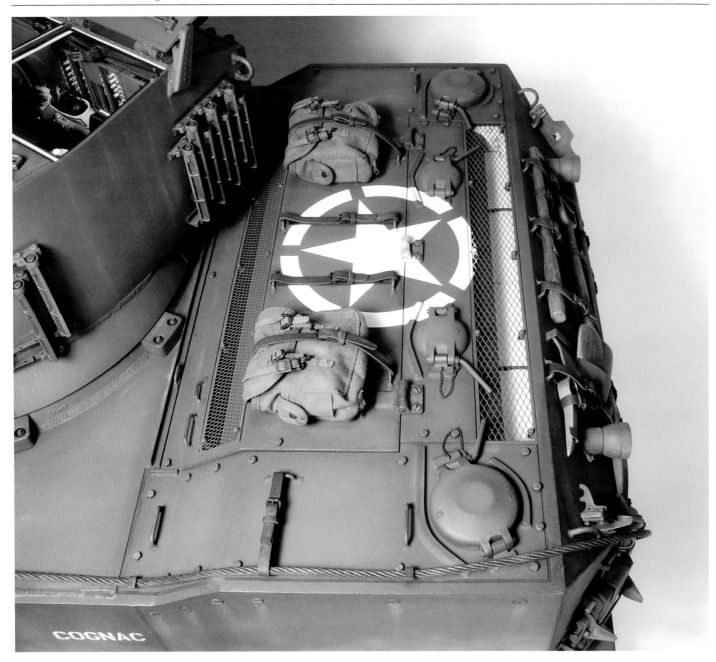

Details of the engine deck show the tow cable clamping brackets and tie-down strap. Two M1936 field packs (Musette bags) were weathered and strapped down. Under the engine hatch is the model's 12 volt battery and volume control.

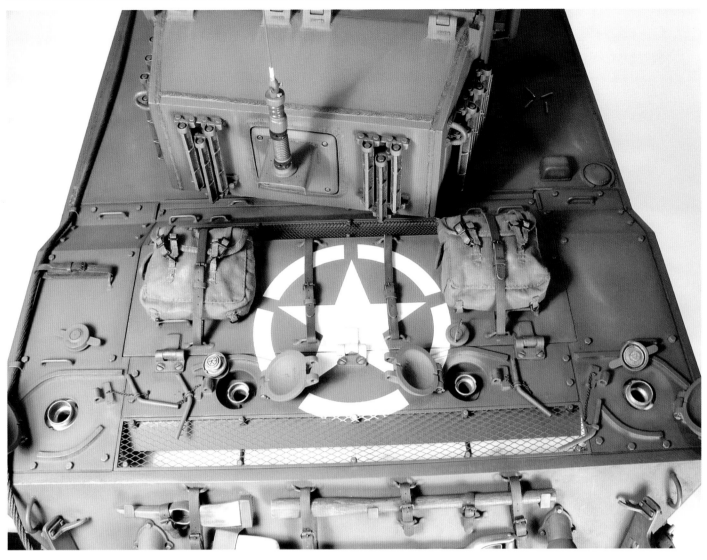

The armor covers for the two fuel tank filler caps (outboard) and the two radiator filler caps (inboard) are open. These operate and secure like the original using locking handles attached by chains to prevent their loss.

The turret hatches are closed and can be locked by the working padlock visible behind the gunner's sight. The lid for the ammo box is on the roof behind the spotlight.

The hatch operating handles operate sliding bars which lock the hatches in the open position. The grousers bolt up to the welded-on racks and can be removed.

The turret has a full interior, including the SCR-508 FM radio in the turret bustle. A M1928A1 .45 caliber Thompson sub-machine gun is stowed on top of the radio.

The periscopes swivel as per the original and have two reflectors and cover glass on both the upper and lower ends. The M6 37mm gun breech has a working breech block.

An M1911A1 .45 caliber automatic pistol lies on the gunner's seat with the slide locked open. Headsets and throat microphones are provided for crewmembers, along with rations and cigarettes. The four white hatch locking handles at the forward edge of the hatch openings operate like the originals.

The M1919A1 .30 caliber machine gun swivels, the locking handle on the quadrant can be loosened to allow the gun to elevate, and the fine-adjustment elevation and windage knobs under the gun's receiver operate.

There are three "live" brass .30 caliber rounds next to the tank commander's periscope on the hull roof, while four empty brass shell cases lie on the hull next to the .30 caliber gun.

Final home for the model is a Plexiglas case for protection from dust, cats, children, and, perhaps most of all, the builder who is often tempted to play with it.

Bibliography

Why so many books?

Quite a few books were used during the course of this project, and this list may seem overly extensive. Not all of them were necessary, strictly speaking, in order to build this model, so I should offer an explanation of why they're listed here. To me this project was more about learning than building a model. By this I mean the education I received from reading about the history of the M5A1 Stuart, its engines, transmissions, guns, tank gunnery, and so on, were as important to me as the building of the model itself. In a sense, building the model was like having a three-dimensional training aid to help support the understanding of all the tank's components and systems, rather than the usual process of having books to support the building of a model. After almost five years of building and reading I felt I had gotten to know this armored fighting vehicle rather well, and that to me was as much fun as creating the model itself. I've listed all these books for other modelers who may feel the same.

All of the publications listed here pertain to the M5A1 Stuart, either in whole or in part.

Commercial publications

Armored School, The: Tank Department. *Driver's Manual for Light Tanks: M5 and M5A1 Light Tanks, and Carriage, Motor, 75-MM Howitzer, M8*. Fort Knox, Kentucky: The United States Army Armored School, 1944. (Reprint by Portrayal Press)

Berndt, Thomas. *American Tanks of World War II*, Chapter 3: *Light Tanks*. Osceola, Wisconsin: MBI Publishing Company, 1994.

Cadillac Motor Car Division, General Motors Corporation. *Driving Instructions-Light Tank, M5, M5A1; Motor Carriage, M8*. Detroit, Michigan: 1942. (Reprint by Portrayal Press)

Crow, Duncan. *Armoured Fighting Vehicles in Profile, Volume 4: American AFVs of World War II*, Chapter 1: Ellis, Chris, and Peter Chamberlain, *Light Tanks M1-M5*. Windsor, Berkshire, UK: Profile Publications Ltd., 1972.

Doyle, David. *M5 AND M5A1 STUART LIGHT TANK-A PHOTOGRAPHIC STUDY*. Iola, Wisconsin: Crooked Creek Publishing LLC, 2006.

Doyle, David. *AFVISUAL-THE STUART SERIES*. Moscow Mills, Missouri: Letterman Publications, 2006.

Forty, George. *United States Tanks of World War II in Action*; Chapter 3: *Early Light Tanks and Combat Cars*; Chapter 4: *The M3: A 'Honey of A Tank'*; Chapter 5: *The M5: The End of A Line*. Poole, Dorset, UK: Blandford Press, 1983.

Franz, Michael. *U.S. WWII M5 & M5A1 STUART LIGHT TANKS*. Erlangen, Germany: Tankograd Publishing, 2008.

Gander, Terry J. *Light Tank M5 & M5A1–Stuart VI & M8 HMC*, Tanks in detail 8. Hersham, Surrey, UK: Ian Allen Publishing, 2004.

Halberstadt, Hans. *Inside The Great Tanks*, Chapter 2: *World War II, M5A1 Stuart*. Marlborough, Wiltshire, UK: The Crowood Press Ltd., 1997. (Six pages of exterior and interior color photos of an M5A1)

Hughes, Chris. *M5A1 Stuart Walkaround CD*. San Jose, California: Toadman's Tank Pictures in conjunction with Tiger Model Designs, 2005.

Hunnicutt, R. P. *Stuart–A History of the American Light Tank*. Novato, California: Presidio Press, 1992. (This may be considered the "Bible" of Stuart tank references. Highly recommended, and you may consider yourself very fortunate if you find a copy. At any price.)

Laughlin, Kurt. *A Field Guide to the M5 Series Light Tanks and the M8 Howitzer Motor Carriage*. Self-published, 2008. (An excellent guide to unraveling the Stuart's many differences and permutations.)

Mesko, Jim. *U.S. Armor Camouflage and Markings World War II*. Carrollton, Texas: Squadron/Signal Publications, Inc., 2005. (Numerous photos and color profiles of various Stuart variants: recommended)

Mucha, Krzysztof, and George Parada. *M5A1 Stuart*, Kagero 18. Lublin, Poland: Kagero, 2003.

Perrett, Bryan. *The Stuart Light Tank Series*, Vanguard 17. London, UK: Osprey Publishing Ltd, 1980.

Schreier, Konrad F. Jr. *Standard Guide to U.S. World War II Tanks & Artillery*, Chapter 1: *The Stuart Light Tanks*. Iola, Wisconsin: Krause Publications, 1994.

Zaloga, Steven J. *Stuart–U.S. Light Tanks in action*, Armor No. 18. Carrollton, Texas: Squadron/Signal Publications, Inc., 1979.

Zaloga, Steven J. *US Light Tanks at War 1941-45*. Hong Kong, China: Concord Publications Company, 2001.

Zaloga, Steven J. *M3 & M5 Stuart Light Tank 1940-45*, New Vanguard 33. Botley, Oxford, UK: Osprey Publishing Ltd, 1999.

Zaloga, Steven J. *Modelling the M3/M5 Stuart Light Tank*, Osprey Modelling 4. Botley, Oxford, UK: Osprey Publishing Ltd, 2003. (An excellent primer on building several different Stuarts in 1/35 scale: highly recommended)

Military field and technical manuals

A.F.V. Publications Section. *Vehicle Training Pamphlet (Provisional), STUART VI (M5A1)*. A.F.V. School: Bovington Camp, Dorset, UK, April 1945.

Hamilton Ordnance Depot. *M5 STUART LIGHT TANK HULL & TURRET ASSEMBLY MANUAL*. No location given: 1988.

Headquarters, Department of the Army. Technical Manual *TM 9-1005-212-12P, OPERATOR AND ORGANIZATIONAL MAINTENANCE REPAIR PARTS AND SPECIAL TOOL LISTS, MACHINE GUNS, CALIBER .30, M1917A1, M1919A4, AND*

M1919A6; MOUNTS,TRIPOD, MACHINE GUN, M1917A1 AND M2; AND MOUNT, TRIPOD, MACHINE GUN-RIFLE, M74. Washington, D.C.: United States Government Printing Office, JULY 1964.

U.S. Army Ordnance Department. *ENGINEERING DRAWINGS-M5/M5A1 STUART LIGHT TANK 331 PLATES*. Washington, D.C.: U.S. Army Ordnance Department, November 22, 1943.

U.S. War Department. Technical Manual *TM 9-732 Light Tanks M5 and M5A1*. Washington, D.C.: United States Government Printing Office, 27 NOVEMBER 1943. (Reprint by Portrayal Press)

U.S. War Department. Technical Manual *TM 9-1727B ORDNANCE MAINTENANCE, ENGINE COOLING, ENGINE ELECTRICAL AND ENGINE FUEL SYSTEMS FOR LIGHT TANK M5 AND 75-MM HOWITZER MOTOR CARRIAGE M8*. Washington, D.C.: United States Government Printing Office, January 4, 1943.

U.S. War Department. Technical Manual *TM 9-1727C ORDNANCE MAINTENANCE, HYDRA-MATIC TRANSMISSION and PROPELLER SHAFTS for LIGHT TANKS M5, M5A1, and 75-MM HOWITZER MOTOR CARRIAGE M8*. Washington, D.C.: United States Government Printing Office February 5, 1943.

U.S. War Department. Technical Manual *TM 9-1727D ORDNANCE MAINTENANCE, TRANSFER UNIT FOR LIGHT TANKS M5, M5A1, AND 75-MM HOWITZER MOTOR CARRIAGE M8*. Washington, D.C.: United States Government Printing Office, April 28, 1943.

U.S. War Department. Technical Manual *TM 9-1727E ORDNANCE MAINTENANCE, CONTROLLED DIFFERENTIAL, FINAL DRIVE, TRACKS AND SUSPENSION FOR LIGHT TANKS M5, M5A1, AND 75-MM HOWITZER MOTOR CARRIAGE M8*. Washington, D.C.: United States Government Printing Office, 25 JUNE, 1943.

U.S. War Department. Technical Manual *TM 9-1727G ORDNANCE MAINTENANCE, HULL AND TURRET FOR LIGHT TANKS M5, M5A1, AND 75-MM HOWITZER MOTOR CARRIAGE M8*. Washington, D.C.: United States Government Printing Office, 3 AUGUST 1943.

U.S. War Department. Technical Manual *TM 9-1729A ORDNANCE MAINTENANCE, LIGHT TANKS M5, M5A1, 75-MM HOWITZER MOTOR CARRIAGE M8, AND TWIN 40-MM GUN: ENGINES, COOLING SYSTEMS AND FUEL SYSTEMS*. Washington, D.C.: United States Government Printing Office, 28 NOVEMBER 1944.

U.S. War Department. Basic Field Manual *FM 23-81 37-MM GUN, TANK, M6 (MOUNTED IN TANKS)*. Washington, D.C.: United States Government Printing Office, APRIL 3, 1942.

U.S. War Department. Technical Manual *TM 9-1250 ORDNANCE MAINTENANCE, 37-MM Gun MATÉRIAL (TANK) M5 AND M6*. Washington, D.C.: United States Government Printing Office, MARCH 10, 1942.

U.S. War Department. Technical Manual *TM 11-600 RADIO SETS SCR-508-A, C, D, AM, CM, DM; SCR-528A, C, D, AM, CM, DM; and AN/VCR-5*. Washington, D.C.: United States Government Printing Office, May 1947.

U.S. War Department. Technical Manual *TM 11-2720 INSTALLATION OF RADIO AND INTERPHONE EQUIPMENT IN LIGHT TANKS M5 AND M5A1*. Washington, D.C.: United States Government Printing Office, DECEMBER 1944.

U.S. War Department. Field Manual *FM 17-12 TANK GUNNERY*. Washington, D.C.: United States Government Printing Office, April 22, 1943.

U.S. War Department. Field Manual *FM 17-68, ARMORED CREW DRILL, LIGHT TANK M5 SERIES*. Washington, D.C.: United States Government Printing Office, 24 May 1944.

U.S. War Department. Basic Field Manual *FM 23-50, BROWNING MACHINE GUN .30, HB, M1919A4 (MOUNTED IN COMBAT VEHICLES)*. Washington, D.C.: United States Government Printing Office, AUGUST 12, 1942.

Sources, Suppliers, and Online Resources

Sources and suppliers that were used for this project–valid as of 28 May 2011

3M: Acryl Green Body putty.
http://www.3m.com/product/information/Acryl-Green-Spot-Putty.html

6th Scale Icons, Inc.: Photoetch padlocks.
http://www.6thscaleicons.com/

AMACO: Copper WireForm wire mesh in 1/8" and 1/16" for the air deflectors and engine screening.
http://www.amaco.com

Archer Fine Transfers: Waterslide resin details: "Casting symbols (foundry marks) 1/35, 1/48 and 1/72", AR88007.
http://www.archertransfers.com/

Armorpax: Cast white metal aftermarket accessories.
http://www.armorpax.com

Bare Metal Foil Company: Self-adhesive foil in aluminum and other metal colors.
http://www.bare-metal.com/

Berol Prismacolor: Artist's pencils in silver and other colors.
http://www.prismacolor.com/home

Colour Shapers: Artist's tool which blends colors and creates realistic weathering.
http://www.colourshaper.com/

Detail Master: Braided steel wire, model wire in various diameters and colors.
http://www.detailmaster.com/

Dragon in Dream Corporation (DiD): Cast metal Browning .30 caliber machine guns, tripod, belted ammunition, uniform, M1936 field packs (Musette bags), weapons, and stowage items.
http://www.onlinedid.com/

Dragon Models USA, Inc.: Browning M1919A4/A6 .30 caliber machine gun plastic kit.
http://www.dragonusaonline.com/

Dremel: Power hobby tools and accessories.
http://www.dremel.com/

Evergreen Scale Models: Sheet, strip, & rod styrene.
http://www.evergreenscalemodels.com

Floquil: Paint.
http://www.testors.com/category/133504/Floquil

Formations Models: Cast resin tracks.
http://www.formationsmodels.com

GetStencils.com: Custom-made vinyl stencils for markings.
http://www.getstencils.com/

Grafix Friskit Film: Artist's friskit film for making stencils.
http://www.grafixarts.com/product/Frisket_Film

K & S Engineering: Brass tubing, rod, sheet, & strip.
http://www.ksmetals.com/

Kit Kraft, Inc.: Styrene letters, various sizes, for foundry casting marks.
http://www.kitkraft.biz

Lion Roar: 1/35 Metal Numbers & Letters kit LNR-LAM042, 1/6 WWII U.S. Army Military.
http://www.dragonmodelsusa.com/dmlusa/prodd.asp?pid=LNRLAM042

MetalsDepot: Brass bar stock, round, 1" diameter.
http://www.metalsdepot.com

Microfasteners: Brass bolts, nuts, & washers.
http://www.microfasteners.com

Micro-Mark: Taps, tap drills, clearance drills, nut drivers, scribing tool.
http://www.micromark.com

Milliput: Two-part epoxy putty in various colors.
http://www.milliput.com/

Pacer Technology: Cyanoacrylate adhesives.
http://www.supergluecorp.com/zap-brand-products

Panavise: Hobby vise in various models.
http://www.panavise.com/

Panzerwerk: Cast resin accessories.
http://www.panzerwerk.com

Plastruct, Inc.: Structural shapes in plastic.
http://www.plastruct.com/

Preac Tool Co.: Machinist's vise, Micro-Precision Table Saw.
http://www.preac.com

Rio Rondo Enterprises: Leather lace and photoetch buckles to make tie-down straps.
http://www.riorondo.com/

Schumo-Kit: Aluminum 37 mm gun barrels and barrel adapter:
http://www.axels-modellbau-shop.de

Sherline Products, Inc.: Modeler's lathe.
http://www.sherline.com/

The Small Shop: Maker of the 'Hold and Fold' photoetch bending tool.
http://www.thesmallshop.com/

SnJ Spray Metal: An excellent paint and metal powder system which replicates metal.
http://hawkeyes-squawkbox.com

Testors Corporation: Glue, paint.
http://www.testors.com/

Waldron: Precision Punch & Die set.
http://www.rollmodels.com

Walthers: Brass bolts, nuts, & washers.
http://www.walthers.com

Windsor & Newton: Artist's oil paints.
http://www.winsornewton.com/

Woodland Scenics: Dry transfer unit markings: MG740 45° USA GOTHIC WHITE LETTERS, & MG727 GOTHIC RAILROAD WHITE NUMBERS.
http://woodlandscenics.woodlandscenics.com/index.cfm
X-ACTO: X-TRA Hands, hobby knives, tools, accessories.
http://www.xacto.com/

Online resources-1/6 scale items, forums, and information-valid as of 28 May 2011
6th Scale Icons: Home-A U.S. manufacturer of German WWII armor accessories.
http://www.6thscaleicons.com/
Armortek: A UK manufacturer of metal armor kits.
http://www.armortek.co.uk/
East Coast Armory: A U.S. manufacturer of armor accessories.
http://www.eastcoastarmory.com/
Field of Armor: A U.S. manufacturer of metal armor kits.
http://www.fieldofarmortanks.com/
G103 Yahoo Group: A forum of enthusiasts dedicated to the study of the Stuart tank. Joe DeMarco's *M5 AND M5A1 SERIAL NUMBER AND REGISTRATION NUMBER ASSIGNMENTS* may be found here as an Excel spread sheet in the Files section once you've registered and have become a member.
http://groups.yahoo.com/group/G103/
Gary's Military Modelling Pages: Links to many 1/6 scale armor and figure sites of interest.
http://johkaz.byethost16.com/forums.html
Kampfgruppe von Abt: A UK-based site devoted to 1/6 scale dioramas incorporating armor, aircraft, figures, locomotives, artillery, and devastated towns. Superior photography, excellent models; this site will inspire you to start your own 1/6 scale model.
http://www.vonabt.co.uk/
M5stuarttankbattalion: A Yahoo discussion group devoted to the 21st Century Toys M5A1 Stuart. The site contains information on the model's repair, maintenance, and many photos of members' models.
http://groups.yahoo.com/group/M5Stuartrctankbattalion/

Newthorpe Models: A UK-based full-service site offering accessories, painting, kits, and refurbishment of models.
http://www.newthorpemodels.co.uk/
Onesixthhobby.com: A French online supplier of kits, accessories, and figures.
http://www.onesixthhobby.com/
Onesixthwarriors.com: A U.S. forum devoted to all aspects of the 1/6 scale hobby.
http://www.onesixthwarriors.com/forum/front-page-news/
Paulstiger1.com: A UK modeler takes you through the build of his various 1/6 scale armored fighting vehicles.
http://www.paulstiger1.co.uk/index.htm
Plastic Panzers: A U.S. manufacturer of kits and accessories.
http://www.plasticpanzers.8k.com/
Scribd.com: An online repository of millions of books and documents. Many technical and field manuals pertaining to the Stuart (and other armored vehicles) may be downloaded for free once you've uploaded a file of your own in trade.
http://www.scribd.com
Sixth Army Group: A U.S. forum devoted to all aspects of the 1/6 hobby. Highly recommended!
http://www.sixtharmygroup.com/forums/
Sixty Driver: An excellent U.S. modeler's Web site illustrating his vehicles and figures.
http://www.sixtydriver.com/
Stinch's 1/6 Scale Tiger 1: A U.S. modeler takes the reader on a complete and thorough build of his Armortek Tiger 1.
http://stinch.com/one6armor/index.html
The Panzer Trap: Tim Bowman, a U.S. supplier of accessories, also showcases his excellent 1/6 scale models.
http://thepanzertrap.com/
The Sixth Division: A U.S. forum for all aspects of the 1/6 hobby.
http://onesixthnet.yuku.com/
Vince Abbott: Expert British model builder's photo gallery of armor and figures.
http://vincesgallery.smugmug.com/Hobbies
Willy's RC Models: A U.S. supplier of kits, accessories, and service, including the 21st Century M5A1 Stuart tank.
http://www.customrcmodels.com/M5Stuart/index.htm

About the Author

The author leans on his Agusta A-109C helicopter atop a Minneapolis hospital helipad.

Bob Steinbrunn started modeling at the age of six and has been at it ever since. Bob's models were primarily 1/48 scale aircraft, and he has won a number of first place awards at IPMS/USA National competitions with these. He has written over thirty articles for *FineScale Modeler* magazine describing the building of his models. In his professional life Bob is a pilot flying an Agusta A-109 helicopter in emergency medical service for a hospital.

Later on Bob started building model ships from wood, brass, styrene, and britannia pewter. His 1/192 scale model of the World War II *Fletcher*-class destroyer USS *Kidd* won the Best in Show award at the Mariners Museum ship model competition in Newport News, Virginia, in 2000, the Best in Show award at the Wisconsin Maritime Museum at Manitowoc in 2001, and the Best in Show award at the IPMS/USA Nationals in Kansas City in 2006. Bob has written over twenty articles for *Ships in Scale* magazine and the Nautical Research Journal.

Left: *FineScale Modeler* magazine (September 2001) carrying an article on the author's 1/192 scale model of the World War II *Fletcher*-class destroyer USS *Kidd*.

Right: *Seaways' Ships in Scale* magazine which carried the author's article on the building of his 1/192 scale model of the World War II *Fletcher*-class destroyer USS *Kidd* over five successive issues.

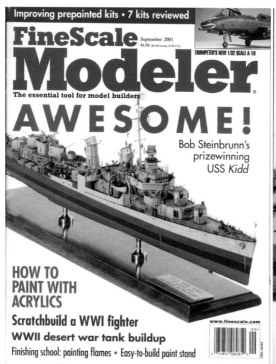

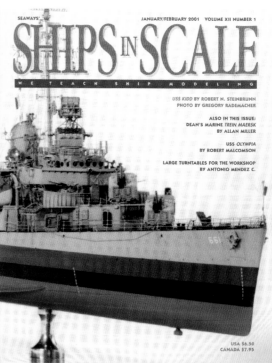

Bob was trained in the U.S. Army as a combat helicopter pilot and served in Vietnam during 1967-1968. He flew UH-1C Huey gunships and UH-1H Huey "slicks" during the year he was there. He has written *Vietnam Scrapbook* for Squadron/Signal Publications about that experience, which is illustrated with more than 200 photographs he took. After leaving the military Bob stayed in civil aviation as a helicopter pilot for the remainder of his career. In 2005 he was honored by being inducted into the Minnesota Aviation Hall of Fame.

Bob's interest in tanks began in 1967 after graduating as a pilot from Army flight school. He was assigned to Ft. Knox, Kentucky, home of the United States Army Armor Center. During the six months he was there–during which time his unit formed up prior to its shipping out for service in Vietnam–Bob became closely involved with armor. He was able to drive several models of tanks (M48A2C, M60A1) on road marches and was able to fire on the main gun range at night. This experience piqued Bob's interest in armor which continues to this day. The photograph of Bob climbing on an M5A1 illustrates the beginning of his association with the Stuart light tank.

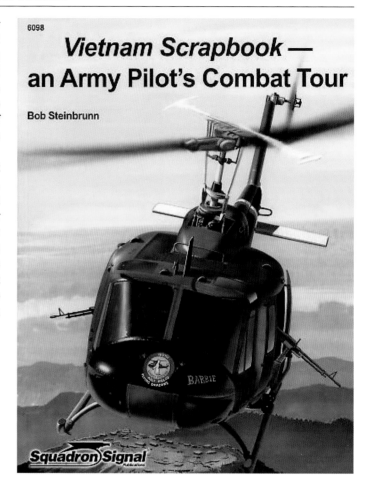

6098

Vietnam Scrapbook — an Army Pilot's Combat Tour

Bob Steinbrunn

BARBIE

Squadron Signal

The author's book released by Squadron/Signal Publications pertaining to his year as a combat helicopter pilot in Vietnam.

A younger (and thinner) Bob climbs on an M5A1 at Ft. Knox, Kentucky, in 1967, beginning his association with the Stuart light tank.

Copyrights

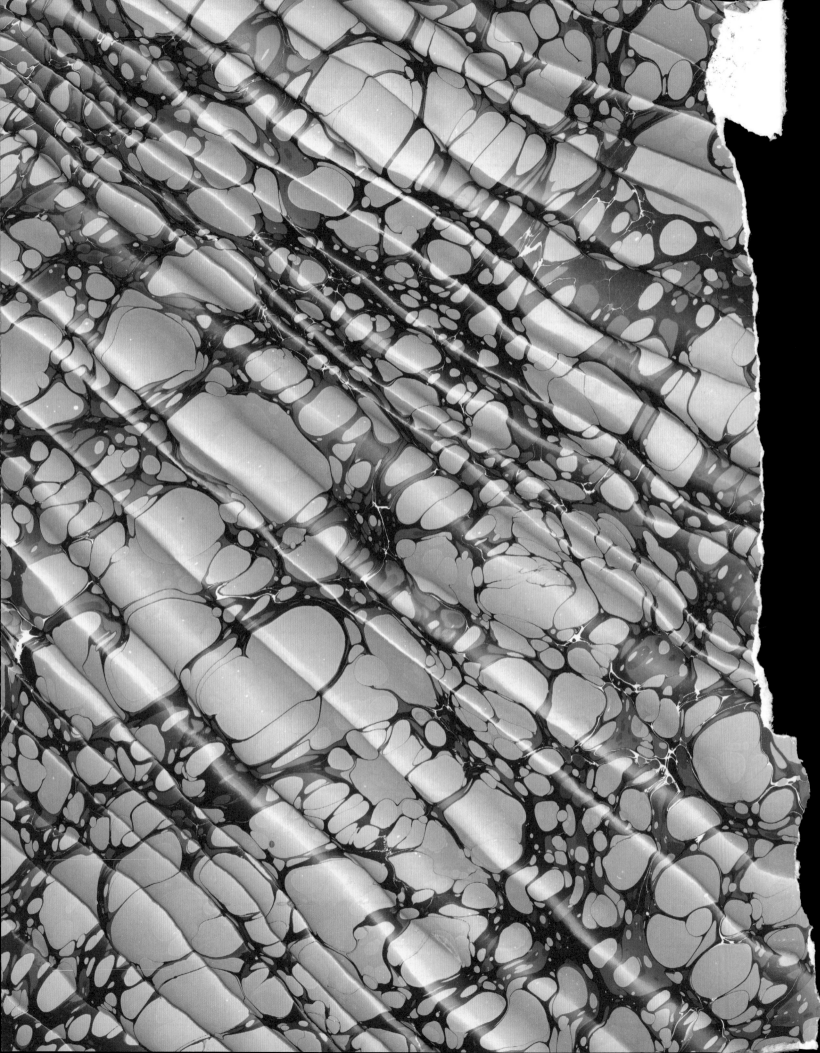